CARVED IN GRANITE

Holocaust Memorials in Greater New York Jewish Cemeteries

ALVIN M. POPLACK

© Copyright 2003 by Alvin M. Poplack.
All rights reserved. Printed in the United States of America.
No part of this book may be transmitted or reproduced
by any means, electronic or mechanical, without written permission,
except for quotations included in reviews.

Published by Jay Street Publishers
155 West 72nd Street, New York, NY 10023

ISBN 1-889534-48-X

Library of Congress

In Everlasting Memory of

LIBBY STRAUSS

צירל בת יצחק הלוי

and

MARTIN STRAUSS

מענדל בן מיכאל הלוי

Pleasant to Everyone
Respected by All
Beloved by Children and Grandchildren

הנאהבים והנעימים בחייהם

They Served Sincerely and Devotedly
As Officers and Stalwart Supporters
of the
INTERNATIONAL SYNAGOGUE
at
John F. Kennedy International Airport

May Their Memories
Be for a Blessing

תנצב"ה

For Roz

ACKNOWLEDGEMENTS

The research reported here originated in the context of a doctoral disserta-tion defended at the Jewish Teachers Seminary in New York, later to become a division of Touro College. I am indebted to the late Dr. Israel Knox, who supervised that dissertation, and whose comment – *"sui generis"* – spurred me on to further effort and to the completion of this work. Since all of my studies and research were conducted at the same time that I was engaged in my full-time duties as pulpit rabbi in a large community, I feel doubly appreciative of Dr. Knox's encouragement.

My sincerest thanks are due to the outstanding scholars, authors and historians of the Holocaust who have endorsed this volume: Professor Elie Weisel, Dr. Irving Greenberg, Rabbi Herschel Schacter, Professor Yaffa Eliach, Dr. Michael Berenbaum, Rabbi Marvin Hier, Mr. Benjamin Meed and Rabbi Bernhard Rosenberg. I consider these endorsements to be the highest of compliments.

On a practical level, I record my gratitude to Ms. Michelle Maslow, without whose generosity this work would not have seen the light of day. She is a true and faithful daughter of Libby and Martin Strauss, of blessed memory, to whom this book is dedicated.

I am particularly grateful to my publisher, Abner E. Kohn, of Jay Street Publishers in New York. From an acquaintance he has turned into a friend. An expert in the field, his guidance has been inestimable. His encouragement and support have strengthened my resolve to see this work come to completion.

I wish to express my gratitude to Rabbi Moses L. Schwab, son of Rabbi Simon Schwab, z"l, for permission to reprint the moving Kinah composed by his father in 1959. I also thank Rabbi Avrohom Biderman of Mesorah Publications, Ltd. for permission to use their translation of the elegy. The addition of this poem to my book brings to it a spirit of deep reverence.

My daughter, Dr. Shana Poplack, Canada Research Chair in Linguistics, and Distinguished University Professor at the University of Ottawa in Ontario, Canada, was indispensable in the production of this volume. She became my unappointed editor – reading the entire manuscript, offering valuable suggestions, correcting errors in language and style and generally bringing to bear her experience as author and editor of several volumes of her own in order to to help ensure the success of her Dad's endeavor. Heartfelt thanks are due her.

The beautiful and expressive cover of this book is the work of my daughter, Miriam Steinberg, of MSteinberg Design in Woodmere, New York. Her skills in the field are clearly evident in her attractive and meaningful production. I thank her for a labor of love.

The promotion and distribution of this book will be in the hands of my son, Ariel, of Plantation, Florida. His organization abilities are well known, and I am fortunate to be the recipient of them.

Many people were consulted during my investigations, research and collecting of material – too numerous to mention. I am, however, particularly grateful to Howard Kotkin, Robert Sherman and Pat Falletta, Directors of Gutterman Funeral Homes, who have gone out of their way to collect and provide me with cemetery maps and locations of Holocaust monuments. Joel Morris, Executive Vice-President of I. J. Morris Chapels, was especially helpful. All have earned my thanks.

Finally, my beloved wife, Roz, is the one who, above all, deserves my appreciation and gratitude. Many were the times that I was ready to shelve this project, pleading lack of time, exhausting schedules and other lame excuses. Throughout my long career in the rabbinate and in the chaplaincy, she has been more than an "ayzer k'negdo" (a faithful helpmate). She was always speaking words of encouragement, of constructive criticism and, above all, of wise counsel. Her trait of perseverance was a constant source of strength and an impetus toward excellence in accomplishment.

How skilled she became in managing our family life and in conducting a traditional home for our three children and a busy husband is surely noteworthy. Furthermore, at the same time, she was involved in her career as a talented and highly successful teacher of the hearing impaired, literally bringing life to numerous handicapped children. Roz excelled in both fields. To her go my undying gratitude and boundless thanks. May we be blessed by the Almighty with many more years, side by side, in continued health and happiness.

Alvin M. Poplack
April, 2003

Michael H. Steinhardt
Chairman

Rabbi Irving Greenberg, Ph.D.
President

Jonathan J. Greenberg
Executive Director

December 5, 2002

Rabbi Alvin Poplack
13700 SW 11th Street
Plymouth A-201
Pembroke Pines, FL 33027

This book constitutes a remarkable act of love and memory. Rabbi Alvin Poplack has scoured the cemeteries in the New York-New Jersey area and recorded (classified and photographed) the memorials erected for the Six Million or for specific town populations and groups who were murdered by the Nazis. For the vast majority of the Six Million there are no markers or graveside memorials; they were denied the dignity of burial. Out of love, various landsmanschaften and individuals put up memorials/markers in local cemeteries to preserve the names of the communities, or in some causes the names of individuals who perished. Now Rabbi Poplack has uncovered these neglected, often hidden away monuments and memorials and put them before the public in this precious book. To rescue the memory of a human being from oblivion is one of the greatest mitzvahs there is – and this volume is a holy book.

Rabbi Irving Greenberg
President, Jewish Life Network

Jewish Life Network
STEINHARDT FOUNDATION
6 East 39th Street 10th Floor
New York, NY 10016
Phone: 212-279-2288
Fax: 212-279-1155

A JUDY AND MICHAEL STEINHARDT FOUNDATION

DR. MICHAEL BERENBAUM
1124 South Orlando Avenue
Los Angeles, California 90035
(323) 930-9325 Phone
(323) 935-9056 Fax
michael@berenbaumgroup.com

February 9, 2003

Rabbi Alvin M. Poplack
13700 SW 11th Street
Plymouth A-201
Pembroke Pines, Florida 33027

Dear Rabbi Poplack:

Thank you for sharing a copy of your book with me. You may use all or part of the following:

> *Etched in Granite* is an important piece of research, documenting, photographing and commenting upon the many memorials to the Shoah that have been erected in the cemeteries surrounding New York, the city with the largest number of Jews in the Diaspora. Many of these memorials were created in the first years after the word of what happened to European Jewry was heard and they represent some of the earliest attempt to give voice to the most important Jewish catastrophe since the exile from Jerusalem, an atrocity that does not easily lend itself to religious language in memorials that was erected in places of religious significance where the earthly confronts eternity. As such, it is a significant – dare one say essential and indispensable – contribution to the process by which we understand memorialization and memory of the Holocaust. It documents the tribute that the generation that was lucky enough – perhaps even wise enough – to leave Eastern Europe paid to the parents and siblings, nieces and nephews they left behind, never to see again, the family that were too late to go forth to an unknown land.
>
> Michael Berenbaum, Director
> Sigi Ziering Institute Exploring the Ethical and Religious Implications of the Holocaust
> Professor of Theology
> Former Project Director and Director of Research Institute
> United States Holocaust Memorial Museum

Congratulations and thank you!

Sincerely yours,

Michael Berenbaum

Prof. Yaffa Eliach
300 East 54ᵗʰ Street, Apt. 23 K
New York City, New York 10022
Phone 212-319-2927
Fax 212-751-7932
shtetlfoundation@prodigy.net

Rabbi Alvin Poplack's book on *Holocaust Memorials in Metropolitan New York Jewish Cemeteries*, is an excellent book and a fundamental key for future generations. The book presents essential information about the murder of the East European City and Shtetl Jews during the Holocaust, and it presents their original hometowns where they lived prior to their murder. The photos in the book present memorial tombstones of the victims located in the many cemeteries that were originally established by immigrants from Eastern Europe.

This magnificent book with its written information and photos of the memorial monuments creates a bridge for present and future generations in order to keep in touch with their Holocaust family victims and their knowledge about their East European roots.

May God bless the people who will cross this special bridge of Rabbi Alvin Poplack's very important book.

All the best,

Prof. Yaffa Eliach

TABLE OF CONTENTS

Introduction / 15

One / *Memorials* / 17

Two / *Major Memorials with Remnant Burial* / 21

Three / *Major Memorials with Extensive Text* / 26

Four / *Large Memorials* / 32

Five / *Self-Sacrifice of Artur Zygelboim* / 48

Six / *Medium Sized Memorials* / 51

Seven / *Small Memorials with Specific Text* / 63

Eight / *Small Memorials with General Text* / 73

Nine / *Organization Monuments which Establish a Date of Yahrzeit* / 78

Ten / *Family Markers which Add Names of Holocaust Martyrs* / 81

Eleven / *Conclusions and Recommendations* / 92

Appendix / 95

Additional Photographs (Appendix 9) / 143

Bibliography / 175

INTRODUCTION

The event which has made the most profound impression on the Jewish People in contemporary times is, without doubt, the Holocaust. Although nearly six decades have elapsed since the first details of the mass extermination of Jews began to trickle out to the world, the magnitude of the plans for genocide, which very nearly succeeded, is such that the passage of time has resulted in greater rather than lesser interest in the Holocaust. Increasingly, major studies are appearing on every aspect of that most gruesome of periods in the history of mankind. That such studies still do not answer the questions which have vexed us through the years in no way minimizes the interest they have generated.

From the very beginning, when the truth began to dawn upon us, nagging questions penetrated deep into our consciousness. How could the destruction of Jews be carried out with such diabolical systemization? How could human beings descend to such depths? How could victims go meekly to their slaughter? Why did the world stand by without halting this destruction?

Now, 56 years after World War II ended, although we may know more of the mind-boggling statistics, we have yet to fathom the answers to the questions which plumb our very depths, which give us no rest. We know that the Third Reich plunged the world into the costliest war in history, in human terms: 35 million people killed, among them almost six million Jews. But we are no closer to knowing why the world was silent while Jews were being slaughtered like cattle, while innocent babes in arms were torn into pieces before the very eyes of their equally innocent mothers.

The bitter truth haunts us. Though the Third Reich fell in ruins, even in defeat Hitler and Nazism were triumphant: the vibrant life of East European Jewry is no more. The lands which nurtured the pulsating communities of thousands of cities, towns and *shtetlach* are now one vast graveyard. A graveyard, alas, without markers.

CHAPTER ONE
MEMORIALS

From the earliest times, memorials have been built to commemorate events or to preserve the memory of great men. The Arc de Triomphe in Paris is a memorial to the victories of Napoleon. In our nation's capital, Washington, D.C., there stand three memorial tributes to great leaders in American history, Washington, Jefferson and Lincoln.

Monuments have been erected on battlefields and at places which are historically important. Gettysburg, Pennsylvania contains a number of such monuments to commemorate a major turning point in the Civil War. Among all locations for memorials, cemeteries are the most common, where a tombstone marks the site of a grave, and epitaphs are inscribed with appropriate texts.

The history of our Jewish people carries it into a Diaspora which is extensive. Jewish communities have sprung up in various countries; indeed, wherever Jews have been permitted to carve out for themselves a domicile and a livelihood. The longevity of such communities has varied wildly. So many years in this land, so many centuries in that. communities sprang up at the whim of medieval princes, and came to an end just as swiftly with an edict of expulsion. For the Jews then a cemetery, even in those lands where Jewish communities existed for centuries, never had a guarantee of permanence.

Where are the cemeteries and where are the markers for the martyrs of *Churban Bayis Sheni* (destruction of the 2nd Temple) in the Jerusalem of the first century? Where are the markers and the burial places of those who perished *al Kiddush Hashem* (for the sanctification of God's Holy Name) in the auto-da-fes of the Inquisition in 15th century Spain? Where are the cemeteries and where are the markers for those who met death when Englishmen set fire to the fortress in York in

1190? And where are the cemeteries and the markers for the Jews of 17th century Poland whom Chmelnitzki's bloodthirsty Cossack hordes put to the sword?

The answer can be found in the Jewish Prayer Book, in the *Sidur* and in the *Machzor*. The introduction to the *Slichos* of Yom Kippur Day is the elegy for the *Asoroh Harugay Malchus*. The *piyutim* of Kol Nidre Night and the fast day following were authored by those who sought to immortalize the martyrs, not in stone, but in the hearts of their descendants. The *Av Harachamim* preceding the *Shabbos Musaf* cries out to the Almighty to avenge the *"spilt blood of Thy servants."* It pleads for remembrance of the upright and innocent who laid down their lives *"al Kiddush HaShem."*

The *Avinu Malkainu,* one of the oldest of all the litanies, was transferred from the High Holy Days to the Ten Days of Repentance, then to fast days, and implores the Almighty's compassion *"for the sake of those slain for Thy Holy Name."* It adds the entreaty *"avenge the blood of Thy servants that hath been shed."*

The lament called *V'hu Rachum* is recited in the Synagogue twice weekly, at the Monday and Thursday morning service, and beseeches God:

> *"P'kach ei-necho u-r'ay shom' mosaynu*
> open Thine eyes and behold our desolations –
> *Habitoh v'a-naynu b'ays tzoroh*
> Look, and answer us in the time of trouble."

The section ends with a soul-stirring cry:

> *"Habayt mee-sho-mayim u-r'ay*
> Look down from Heaven and see how we have become a scorn and derision among the nations; we are considered as sheep brought to the slaughter, to be slain and destroyed . . ."

Despite this strong tradition of memorial through prayer, there are equally strong feelings among Jews that memorials should also be tangible. A visit to any Jewish cemetery will prove the point. There can be seen memorial markers of every size, shape and form.

In Metropolitan New York area cemeteries an entire new

category of monuments bids for our attention. These are monuments to the victims of the Holocaust, erected on United States soil by those whose fervent wish it was that the martyrs never be forgotten.

Who is responsible for erecting these memorials? The overwhelming majority of them have been erected by organizations – *landsmanshaften*. These are societies which were established in America by immigrants who hailed from a specific village, town or vicinity in Europe. Among the functions they fulfilled was contact with their home town and its residents, parents, siblings, family or friends.

When the tragedy of the Holocaust overtook Europe and caused the virtual disappearance of the home town and the destruction of its inhabitants, sorrow and mourning was felt on these shores. Those feelings gave birth to a determination to memorialize for eternity those who perished, in the form of markers identified in this study.

Where were these memorials placed? The answer comes from another of the functions the *landsmanshaften* fulfilled – to provide burial ground for its members. It was upon these organizational burial grounds that the memorials were erected.

The inscriptions on these monuments run the gamut from the most elaborate to the very simple. Some are detailed, some are general. Some are huge, some are tiny. Some mention the oppressor explicitly, some leave it to the reader's imagination. Some are only in Hebrew, some only in Yiddish, some only in English. Others are in all three languages.

A small number of such memorials has been erected by families that have no connection with any organization. There is also a trend toward adding onto a personal monument a text in memory of specific Holocaust victims. In what follows we shall see examples of them all.

Where are these monuments and memorials? That is the question this study set out to answer. Prior to the research presented here, there was no record of them, even at the cemeteries where they stand. Inquiries at cemetery offices and monument companies were fruitless. The largest compendium of *landsmanshaften* organizations is kept by the United Jewish Appeal. In response to a request for the list of organizations which had erected memorials, the writer was informed that such lists are not customarily made available. Inquiry at the YIVO Institute for Jewish Research also produced a negative response.

The answer to the question of where the memorials are was finally provided by my own observation. Over a period of several years, in visits to the cemeteries listed, and others, memorials were discovered and recorded. Questions put to grave diggers employed at the cemeteries produced some results, but not nearly enough. The information which follows is, in large measure, the product of the author's legwork, his personal, persistent investigation and his camera. Let these monuments now speak for themselves.

CHAPTER TWO
MAJOR MEMORIALS WITH REMNANT BURIAL

Outstanding among the memorials to Holocaust victims erected on the grounds of cemeteries are three monuments. They are singled out for attention not only because they are large and imposing. They draw attention to themselves for a compelling reason – at the base of each of them is buried the only tangible remnants of the era of mass murder of Jews. That remnant is the ashes of those put to death, brought over to the United States from the crematory at Auschwitz. These ashes lie at the base of two memorials. At the third is buried an object which is a grim reminder of human depravity at its worst – a bar of soap manufactured by the Nazis from the bodies of their Jewish victims.

In terms of the stark horror evoked by the monuments to the Holocaust as a group, the memorial erected by the First Zbarazer Relief Society at Beth David Cemetery in Elmont, Long Island, is primary. That bar of soap sums up, in and of itself, the fiendish brutality of the Nazi oppressors, a fiendishness that knew no bounds, that pursued its victims not only to the gates of death itself but beyond it. Rarely has there been recorded in the annals of civilization a violation of human dignity so great in its magnitude.

On Long Island, at the base of the Zbarazer monument, is the object, both holy and horrible – soap made from the bodies and fats of the Jewish marytrs, given here the reverential burial accorded to the dead in the Jewish tradition. Suitably marked, the site now serves as a final resting place for those nameless martyrs whose bodies were violated in so loathsome a manner.

Of the eighty-six monuments included in this study, the Zbarazer burial of the bar of soap is the very first, having been dedicated on September 7, 1947. Providentially, Jewish burial, previously denied these martyrs, is now their eternal inheritance.

The monument erected by the First Zbarazer Relief Society is a tall monument in the form of a four-sided obelisk (Figures 1 and 2). On the front is the text in English, which is dedicatory and descriptive of the specific events which brought to an end the existence of the Jewish community of Zbaraz in Poland.

Of all the samples, this monument is the most detailed, listing the number of Zbaraz Jews "killed" or "murdered, the dates of each action and where they took place. On the back of the monument the text is inscribed in Hebrew. One verse from Scripture (the liturgy) is included: *"Earth, cover not their blood."*

Unfortunately, this monument is hardly visible. Although it is

Figure 1

Figure 2

tall, it is set in the middle of a block in the cemetery. There is very little open space around it, and it is therefore easily overlooked. Indeed, one's eye is hardly drawn to it, and if it is not the object of one's search, it might not be discovered. These facts deserve to be mentioned precisely because the Zbarazer monument tends to be the outstanding one of the entire group. The reasons for this are 1) the burial of the bar of soap; 2) the extensive text, and 3) the specific details of massacre which include places, dates, and number of victims.

The second monument which stands over buried remnants was erected in 1967 by the East Side Social Center of Paterson, New Jersey. It is located in the King Solomon Cemetery in Clifton, New Jersey. It is a very large imposing monument, hexagonal in shape, easily identified because it stands unobstructed on a large plot of ground (Figures 3 and 4). It is recognizable from a distance as a marker of note. The very substantial column is set upon a base which forms a *Mogen David,* the six-sided Jewish star. Around the top are three carved illustrations: a *Menorah*, an Eternal Light and a *Mogen David*.

The text is brief, inscribed on the front in English, to the left side in Hebrew and on the right in Yiddish.

While the Hebrew and Yiddish texts are seemingly translations

Figure 3

Figure 4

of the English, there are subtle yet significant differences which speak volumes. The English text memorializes the *"Six million martyrs killed during the terrible years of the horrors of World War II."* The Yiddish rendering is far more explicit: *"Our six million holy ones, murdered by the bloody hands of the Nazi murderers."* Likewise the Hebrew: *"Our six million holy brothers who were destroyed at the hands of the willfully tyrannous Nazis, may their memories be erased."*

Carved in the middle of the front panel is the form of a tree with its branches cut and falling. In front of this monument is a grave in which the ashes are buried. Over it is a concrete cover on which is inscribed in Yiddish and in English: *"Here rest the ashes of the six million Jewish martyrs taken from the crematory chambers in Auschwitz."*

The major memorial which stands over remnant burial is that erected by the Drobniner Benevolent Society (Figures 5-7). It is located in the United Hebrew Cemetery in Staten Island, New York. This, too, is a tall monument, a four-sided column, surmounted by a *Mogen David*. At its foot is a grave covered by a double concrete slab, on which in Hebrew and in English is a commanding text:

> "Habate! Kever ha-hergah:
> See! The grave of massacre:
> Bo tzorur aifair va-atzoh-mos shel chall'lai ha-k'doshim she-nisfu al y'dai ho-r'sho-im b'mas-ray-fos ho-aish shel Auschwitz.
> Here is bound together ashes and bones of the profaned holy ones who were destroyed by the wicked in the fire-ovens of Auschwitz. Soil . . . cover not their blood!"

This monument deserves attention not only for its imposing size and the large number of names inscribed upon all sides, but also because it is among the relatively few which specify a date of *Yahrzeit*. On the face of the monument is the legend "*Sefer Ha-Chaim* – Book of Life, *Yahrzeit* – 14 Kislev." Thus the Society proclaims a day of memorial in perpetuity for all the Drobniner *landsleit* who perished in the Holocaust. (Figures 5 and 6)

The Yiddish inscription is more descriptive than the English:

> "Tzum ondenk fun unsereh Drobniner k'doshim
> in memory of our beloved Drobniner holy martyrs

velcheh zainen umgeku-men durch dee Deitchishe r'sho-im und zayer mithelfer
who were killed by the German tyrants and their helpers.
Hashem Yikom domom.
May the Almighty avenge their blood."

The inscription in Hebrew over the grave containing the ashes and bones of the martyrs uses the word *"to-mun,"* hidden, a reverential form of "buried." Also etched upon the face of the monument is a replica of the six-branched candelabra at Yad Va Shem, the national Holocaust Memorial in Jerusalem. (Figure 7)

Figure 6

Figure 5

Figure 7

CHAPTER THREE
MAJOR MEMORIALS
WITH EXTENSIVE TEXT

We may now distinguish a second group of major memorials with extensive text. Chief among them is the one erected upon the New Montefiore Cemetery in Pinelawn, Long Island by the Radomer Mutual Society of New York (Figures 8-10). It is among the most beautiful, because its facade is decorated with Jewish symbols: an Eternal Light on each side, and in the middle panel six symbols – the Ten Commandments; a menorah; the symbols which describe the *Kohen* (a pair of hands with fingers outspread in the priestly blessing); those which describe the *Layvee* (a pitcher with water pouring into a basin). Then there is a tree, its full branches cut off at the trunk and falling over, and last, a full set of *seforim*, Jewish books.

These symbols make up the rich tapestry of traditional Jewish communal life. A life, which the monument starkly reminds us, was cut off in its prime, even as was the tree carved into the granite. This tragedy is expressed in words – the Yiddish and Hebrew once again telling a story not found in the English:

> "*Tzum eibiken ondenk*
>   to the eternal memory
> *noch dee eeber dreisig toisend k'doshim*
>   of the more than thirty thousand holy martyrs
> *fun Radom Poilen und umgegend*
>   from Radom Poland and environs
> *velche zainen fargazt, farbrent, und farpeinikt gevoren*
>   who were gassed, burned and brutalized
> *durch dee Daitchen in dee yoren 1939-45*
>   by the Germans in the years 1939-45."

Figure 8

Figure 9

Figure 10

The sides and back of this large monument are covered with the names of martyrs. There is literally not an inch of space left. The vast number of inscriptions bear out the legend that this monument memorializes over 30,000 Radomites annihilated by the Nazis, the largest number mentioned on any monument in this study.

As of this writing this monument, like others, remains partially hidden by its location among many tombstones. Its size and this setting detracts from its inspirational and beautiful workmanship. In its present location the monument is hardly noticeable from the road. It is a pity that one of the most impressive and most meaningful of Holocaust memorials is virtually lost to the public eye, due to lack of open space around it.

Two other large memorials with extensive text are found in the same cemetery, Beth Israel in Woodbridge, New Jersey. One of them is perhaps the most massive of all studied, while the second is among the first to be erected.

The first, Bendin-Sosnowicer, is comprised of three very large pillars surmounted by a granite cover, on the face of which is a text that is a paraphrase of the quotation from the Passover Haggadah, recited by those assembled round the Seder table when the door is opened to welcome Elijah the Prophet. "Pour out Thy wrath upon the nations who know Thee not." (Figures 11-12)

This text is explicit: "Pour out Thy wrath upon the Nazis and the wicked Germans for they have destroyed the seed of Jacob. Pour out

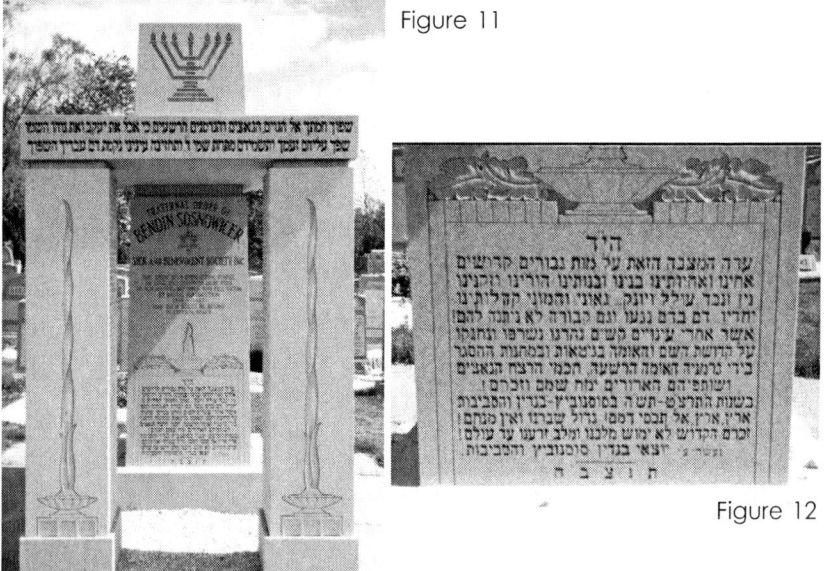

Figure 11

Figure 12

upon them Thy anger, and destroy them from beneath Thy heavens –

V'se-che-zeh-no ay-nay-nu,
    and may our eyes behold,
nik-mas dam a-vo-decho ha-sho-fuch,
    the avenging of Thy servants spilt blood."

The middle pillar contains one of the most expressive texts found on any of the monuments in this study:

"May the Almighty avenge their blood. This monument is a witness to the death of the heroic and righteous brothers and sisters, sons and daughters, parents and grandparents, nieces and nephews, infants and babes in arms, our scholars and our common folk together – their blood ran as one, and even burial was denied them! After terrible persecution they were killed, burned, strangled for the sanctification of the Holy Name and the honor of the Nation.

"This all done in the ghettos and concentration camps by the wicked German people, the master murderers, the Nazis, and their accursed partners, may their memories be blotted out. Occurred in the years 1939-1945 in Sosnowicz-Bendin and environs.

> Earth, earth, refuse to cover their blood!
> Great is our sorrow, and no consolation is to be found!
> Their revered memory will never leave our hearts
> or the hearts of our descendants unto eternity!

The text closes with a pledge that "the memory of these holy martyrs – *lo yomush mee-lee-baynu* – will not be moved from our hearts, and from the hearts of our descendants, forever!"

This striking monument is one of the most visible. Whether by accident or design, it is set in the middle of the Society's plot and, thus far, there are no grave markers between it and the road, easily and readily recognizable as a memorial of some importance.

The second major monument at Beth Israel was erected by the Kolbuszowa Relief Association (Figures 13-15). It was dedicated on June 6, 1948, making it, according to my findings, the second oldest – the first group having been erected in 1947.

It is very large, with a wide central slab flanked by even wider slabs on either side. The front contains an extensive text in English, with a Hebrew translation on the back. Each side slab is covered with the names of martyrs. This memorial is set close to the road so that no other monument can be located in front of it. It is therefore highly visible, and draws attention because of its size.

Anyone stopping to read the text will be struck by the detailed description of the tragedy perpetrated by the Nazis. Once again, we find the Hebrew text much more explicit than the English.

Figure 13

Figure 14

Figure 15

"This monument is
eidoh la-shoah ha-a--yumoh
    witness to the terrifying destruction
ma-a-say y'dai ha-zodone ha-proh-ee
    the handiwork of the wildly wicked
v'ho-resha ha-sa-tany
    and the satanic brutality of the Nazis and those who helped them."

This monument also lists the number of martyrs – one thousand eight hundred – who were put to death in Kolbusov, and described in vivid terms the methods used: "who were destoyed, killed, slaughtered, choked, drowned, burned, and buried alive."

There follows a version of the traditional memorial prayer *"El Molay Rachamim* – O God, full of compassion, grant perfect rest – to all members of their families who were martyred."

Added here is a prayer found only upon some of the other memorials. It is an expression of hope that, in the merit of the martyrs, "may the dispersed of Israel be returned to their borders – *u-v-z'chusom yo-shuvu nidchai yisrael l'gvulom, omain, v'omain.*"

Thus, on this monument the pain and anguish of the death of close family members is channeled into the watchword of Zionism: *"v'shovu vonim l'g'vulom* – may the children be returned to their borders," Jeremiah 31:17.

CHAPTER FOUR
LARGE MEMORIALS

This chapter treats a group of memorials which are generally large in appearance. As compared with the foregoing, however, the text is considerably shorter. Nevertheless, the events described are no less terrifying than those which are memorialized by what I have called the "major" memorials.

We also encounter in this group additional memorialization not directly connected to the Holocaust, in the form of remembrance of sons of members of the Society who served in the United States Armed Forces during World War II and were killed in action. There is some indication here that the Society considered their sacrifice on a level with that of Holocaust victims. On some memorial markers their names are listed and given equal prominence.

Another interesting point emerges from the description of this group of memorials. Generally speaking, nothing in this study indicates any type of joint action to memorialize Holocaust victims by monuments in cemeteries. References always come from Scripture and the liturgy, which is where a Jew would normally look for such quotations. It seemed to me, in all my search, that choice of inscriptions was independently arrived at by each organization.

In this group, however, are three memorials which are identical in style. They were erected by the following societies: Sassower (Figure 16); Orynier (Figure 17); and Yosefov (Figure 18). They seemed to have either been designed by the same person or copied one from another. They are located in Beth Moses and Wellwood Cemeteries in Pinelawn, Long Island which adjoin each other and are under the same ownership (essentially one cemetery).

The memorial by the Wolochisker Benevolent Association erected on their grounds in the Old Montefiore Cemetery in Springfield Gardens, Queens, NY expands the vow of its members that the memory

Figure 16

Figure 17

Figure 18

of the martyrs be kept alive by the Society. It boldly proclaims: "Humanity must never forget them!" This statement is made in the English text but not in the Yiddish beneath it.

On the face of the pillar we find the names of the Monument Committee, while the names of the martyrs are placed on the side. Above the list of martyrs is the name of a son of a member who was killed in action, Captain Fred Sklar (Figure 19).

The Samborer Relief Society Monument on Old Montefiore Cemetery is an obelisk (Figure 20). Its needle reaches up high above the surrounding family markers. It declares, in Hebrew and English, that eight thousand Jews were martyred for *Kiddush HaShem* – sanctification of God's Name.

Figure 19

Figure 20

Figure 21

The Grodner Aid Benevolent Association of New York erected its monument at Mt. Hebron Cemetery in Flushing, NY. In addition to a text in Hebrew and English shown here, there is a meaningful sentence in Yiddish on the back of the monument:

> "*een heiliken ondenk der far-shnee-tener Grodner kehilla*
>   in holy memory of the cut apart Grodner community."
> (Figure 21)

The sheer magnitude of Nazi bestiality is brought forcefully to our attention by the monument of the Rovner Sick and Benevolent Society at Beth David Cemetery in Elmont, Long Island. It tells of the murder of 23,500 Jews by the Nazis on a single day – November 7, 1941! (Figure 22) While this marker is large and thick, and it is directly on the corner of two streets, it is thoroughly undistinguished. No quotation or statement of mourning appears.

Another monument on Beth David Cemetery to an almost equal number of martyrs is that of the Wlodzimierez Society. The text specifies 20,000 men, women and children, and the Hebrew adds the date, 19 Elul 1942. (Figure 23)

Figure 22   Figure 23   Figure 24

The monument of the Rotchever and Voliner Aid Association introduces another element to the memorials we have recorded. The memorial itself, on Old Montefiore Cemetery, is a very tall obelisk with the text on the front in Yiddish, and on the back in English (Figure 24). The first lines are a memorial tribute to

> "*dee heldishe martirer kemfer*
>   the heroic martyrs who were fighters
> *een dee ghettos und lageren*
>   in the ghettos and concentration camps."

Then, it adds "and to our own brothers and sisters of our home town of Rotchev." This represents a type of memorialization that has in this study as yet not been touched upon – a *re*memorialization of those whose tombstone had been destroyed. The text continues:

"*Oich fun dee aleh niftorim*
    and also of all the departed
vas hoben doros lang geruht oifen bais olom
    who have for generations rested in the cemetery
fun unser alter haim
    of our old home town
vos zeireh matzevos zainen op-ge-visht gevoren
    whose tombstones have been wiped out."

The text goes on with a vow: "*mir velen kayn mohl nisht fargesen und fargeben dee Natzishe merder* – we will never forget nor forgive the Nazi murderers who annihilated six million of our Jewish holy martyrs."

This monument, dedicated in 1954, also includes the author's name: "*dee oibendertzailte blutige lahzung far-eibigt fun Louis Yabko* – the above-mentioned bloody events eternalized by Louis Yabko."

Figure 25

This is one of the very few monuments where the name of the author of the text is inscribed. It is also among the few which memorialize the Jews in their hometown who were buried in the community's cemetery which was destroyed by the Nazis. No markers exist for them, and this monument is to serve henceforth as their memorial.

Another in a group of second oldest monuments is that of Antipolia Society on Old Montefiore Cemetery, erected in September 1948. In Hebrew, Yiddish and English we see a brief legend memorializing two thousand five hundred brothers and sisters who were massacred by the Nazis in 1942 and 1943. It is erected base upon base, ending in a small obelisk, (Figure 25). It stands on a corner, nigh to the street, but does not draw attention, because of its dark-colored stone.

Figure 26

The monument of the United Dinewitzer Podolier Benevolent Association was erected in 1965 on their grounds at the New Montefiore Cemetery. Its height and placement, away from other markers, make it prominent. The text is in English and Yiddish, with names of martyrs inscribed on the sides and back (Figure 26).

The English text specifies Nazis and their agents as the murderers. It continues: "Humanity must never forget them," a phrase which is, strangely, not translated in the Yiddish which states: "*mir velen dee heilige korbonos keinmohl nit fargesen* – we will never forget our holy sacrificed martyrs."

Across the street is a monument which commemorates tragedy multiplied – massacre upon massacre. It is the monument erected by the Kieltzer Sick and Benevolent Society of New York in September 1957. The moving legend memorializes 28,000 Jewish martyrs killed in Kielce, Poland within a period of only eight days – from August 20-28, 1942. The monument establishes the date of Yahrzeit to be 9 Elul (Figures 27 and 28).

And, as if this were not enough of a tragedy, on the side we find an additional inscription to memorialize a starkly tragic event – the pogrom upon the survivors of the Nazi death camps who sought to return to their home town of Kielce after the war was ended. They were attacked and killed by Poles on July 4, 1946. Among all our samples this is the single such event recorded.

The Kuzminer–Voliner Young Friends Society erected an imposing memorial on the New Montefiore Cemetery to hundreds of their townfolk who were killed on one day, August 3, 1941. It is a very tall obelisk, towering far above the family markers on the Society's grounds. It is therefore easily seen from the street. (Figures 29 and 30)

Here is a most poignant statement establishing the Yahrzeit:

"Oich velen mir eibig gedenkin
    also will we always remember
dee letzteh verter fun unser alemens rebyn
    the last words of the rebbe of all of us, Ozer Melamed –
az oib emetzer vet blaiben leben
    that if anyone should remain alive
zol gedenken az Tisha B'av 1941 eez der Yahrzeit fun aleh Kuzminer k'doshim

Figure 27

Figure 28

Figure 29

Figure 30

they should always remember that the Fast Day of the Ninth of Av is the Yahrzeit of the martyrs of Kuzmin."

Who among us, reading these lines today, can help but wonder if Reb Ozer Melamed had any doubts that his words would not outlive him?

Also slaughtered on one day were several hundred Jews of Grybow, Galicia. The number of these martyrs was three hundred sixty, and the date of their murder was August 20, 1942. They rest in one common grave, movingly called *"kever achim* – a grave of brothers" and are memorialized at the King Solomon Cemetery in Clifton, New Jersey. This monument (Figure 31) was erected by their American *landsleit*, the Grybower Ladies and Men's Benevolent Society, and was dedicated on September 7, 1947. It is one of the four earliest monuments in this study, inscribed in both Hebrew and in English, and was intended to memorialize the "many sainted martyrs of Grybow," among whom were those who now lie in the "grave of brothers" (Figure 31).

Another marker, erected in 1947, is that of the Rypiner Benevolent Society and is located at Baron de Hirsch Cemetery on Staten Island, New York. While it is also among the four earliest, it is the one which carries the shortest inscriptions – only these words: "In memory of those Rypiner who died at the hands of Nazi tyranny 1939-1945" (Figure 32).

Figure 31

Figure 32

An imposing monument, massive in size, standing boldly among the much smaller family markers, is that of the New Drohobyczer and Boryslawer Benevolent Association at New Montefiore Cemetery (Figure 33). Here we again observe a contrast between the Hebrew text and the English translation. The English seems almost feartureless in its language: "In memory of those who perished for the Sanctification of the Name during the Nazi occupation of Drohobycz and Boryslaw in the years of 1940 to 1945." Contrast this with the literal translation of the Hebrew:

> "*L'zaicher olom yi'hyu ha-k'doshim*
> For eternal memory shall be the holy martyrs, from the town of Drohobycz-Boryslaw
> *she-ne-hergu, v'nis-refu, v'nish-chetu al kiddush ha-Shem*
> who were killed, burned and slaughtered for the Sanctification of the Name of G-d
> *al y'day ha-Natzim*
> at the hands of the Nazis.
> *Ha-Shem Yinkom Domom*
> May the Almighty avenge their blood."

Figure 33

Figure 34

The latter version is far more reflective of events which occurred during the years of the Holocaust.

Figure 34 displays a memorial to four thousand men, women and children of Lechowitz, killed by Nazis on October 29, 1941. This memorial stands in Beth David Cemetery and was erected in October 1961. Here. in contrast to other monuments, more expressive language is used in the English text than in the Yiddish.

> *"Tzum aibiken ondenk*
>   In eternal memory
> *noch dee k'doshim velche zainen gefahlen*
>   of the holy who fell
> *durch dee Natzishe merder*
>   at the hands of the Nazi murderers."

The English version includes this phrase: "Innocently and cruelly slain."

Figure 36A

Figure 35

Figure 36B

Figure 37

Figure 38

Figure 39

The three monuments next described seem to have been fashioned by one hand. Each has four standing pillars surmounted by a horizontal granite bar. In the middle is the form of an altar upon which is an open book. On its pages is the twelfth verse from Chapter Twelve in Lamentations, inscribed in Hebrew and in English translation.

Two of these three memorials contain the same verse:

"*Ha-bitu u-r'u eem yaish mach-ov k'mach-ovee, asher olail lee*
Look. Behold. Is there a pain like ours that befell us."

These two are the Sassower Society at Wellwood Cemetery, (Figure 35), and Otynier Society at Beth Moses Cemetery (Figure 36A), adjoining cemeteries, under the same ownership. It is therefore likely that members of one society saw the monument of the other and found it suitable. It is also possible that a nearby monument maker suggested the plans of one society to the other. The reverse of the horizontal bar also contains the same legend in Hebrew: *"Shofchu domain ka-mayim v'ayn kovair* – Their blood was spilt like water, and there was none to bury them."

On the back of the Otynier memorial is a legend that appears only here among all the monuments of the study. (Figure 36B) With these words, it refers to the many martyrs whose identities were unknown: "In memory of all who perished whose names do not appear and are only known to God."

The Yosefov Society monument at New Montefiore Cemetery (Figure 37) contains a text which is an English rendering of the phrase, *"al Kiddush Ha-Shem* – for the sanctification of God's Name." It is put in the following words: "who perished for their faith and their people." Most texts in this study do not translate *"al Kiddush Ha-Shem"* into English. This makes the phrase understandable to an American Jewish generation which may not know Hebrew. The open book on the altar in this memorial contains a verse from Jeremiah in Hebrew only.

The Kobriner Unterstitzung Verein erected a memorial at Mt. Judah Cemetery which contains a most expressive text in Hebrew (Figure 38). It extols in unusually complimentary terms the "mother city," in these words:

> *"L'naitzach zikaron*
>   In everlasting memory
> *K'doshay Kobrin*
>   the holy martyrs of Kobrin
> *ha-ma-a-teeroh eer v'aym b'yisroel*
>   whose crowning glory was that it was an important city filled with vibrant Jewish life
> *saimel Torah v'chasidus b'Lita*
>   a symbol of Torah and Chassidic lore in Lithuania
> *she-nis-par-semoh b'geoneha v'tzadikeha, raboneha v'admoreha*
>   which was famous for its scholars and righteous ones, for its Rabbis and its Chassidic Rebbes
> *she-nehergu v'nirtz'chu b'ofan tragi*
>   who were murdered and massacred in a tragic fashion –
> *al y'day chaysay teref*
>   at the hands of beasts of prey
> *ha-Natzim ho-arurim*
>   the cursed Nazis – on the eleventh of Av and other times."

Unfortunately, this poignant eulogy is lost to those who cannot read Hebrew. The only English reference is in the form of six words: "In memory of our departed Brethren," which can be easily misunderstood as referring to the members of the Society buried on this plot only.

Figure 40

Thus, the glory of Jewish Kobrin, which was remembered by those who erected this memorial, may be forgotten by the next generation who know not the language of their fathers.

It has been noted that many monuments repeat verses or phrases that are familiar as expressions of mourning, chiefly those from *Aichoh*, the Book of Lamentations. In the text on the monument erected by the Nemirower Immigration and K.U. Verein at Beth David Cemetery we find a singular departure from this practice. It is the only example from all the monuments included in this study.

This text is a paraphrase of Genesis 4:10 in which God speaks to Cain, saying, "The voice of your brother's blood cries out!" In a flight of poetic fancy the text on the Nemirower monument speaks with the voice of the martyrs. It announces (Figure 39):

> "*Kol d'may achaynu tzo-akim aylaynu min ho-adomoh laymor*
>   The voice of our brothers' blood cries out unto us from
>   the earth, saying:
> *Zochor*
>   Remember
> *Al Tish-kach osonu*
>   Do not forget us . . .
> *Harugay Nemirow Rabosi*
>   The martyrs of Nemirow and environs
> s*he-olu al ha-mokad ha-norah*
>   who were sacrificed in the terrible conflagration on four
>   Kislev 1941."

The text in English includes an awesome addition: "Six thousand of the Jews of Nemerow were murdered by the Nazis and their cohorts on a single day, November 24, 1941."

A very large and imposing monument is that erected by the Lodzer Young Men's Benevolent Association at New Montefiore Cemetery. Its size literally dwarfs the individual single headstones (Figure 40). It contains only two words in Hebrew – "*L'zaicher Olam* – In eternal memory" There is also a very short English text which includes two phrases from the Hebrew in English transliteration: "This memorial is dedicated to memory of those who perished *Al Kiddush Ha-Shem* (for the sanctification of God's Name) in the Holocaust with

Shema Yisrael, (Hear O Israel) on their lips. May their souls rest in eternal peace." Mute but eloquent testimony to martyrdom is furnished by long columns on front and back, listing hundreds of names of victims.

This monument, by its sheer size, draws attention to itself. It stands on a plot relatively open, and because it is close to three times the height of an average monument, and four to six times the width, it is highly visible. Due to its size, location and simple English text, it should be considered among the most effective memorials in this study, particularly for English-only speaking people.

One of the first monuments dedicated to the martyrs was erected by the Litiner Podolier Aid Organization and Ladies Auxiliary. It was dedicated in 1947 and is located at Mt. Hebron Cemetery. Several points make it a memorial of note. First, it is one of only four

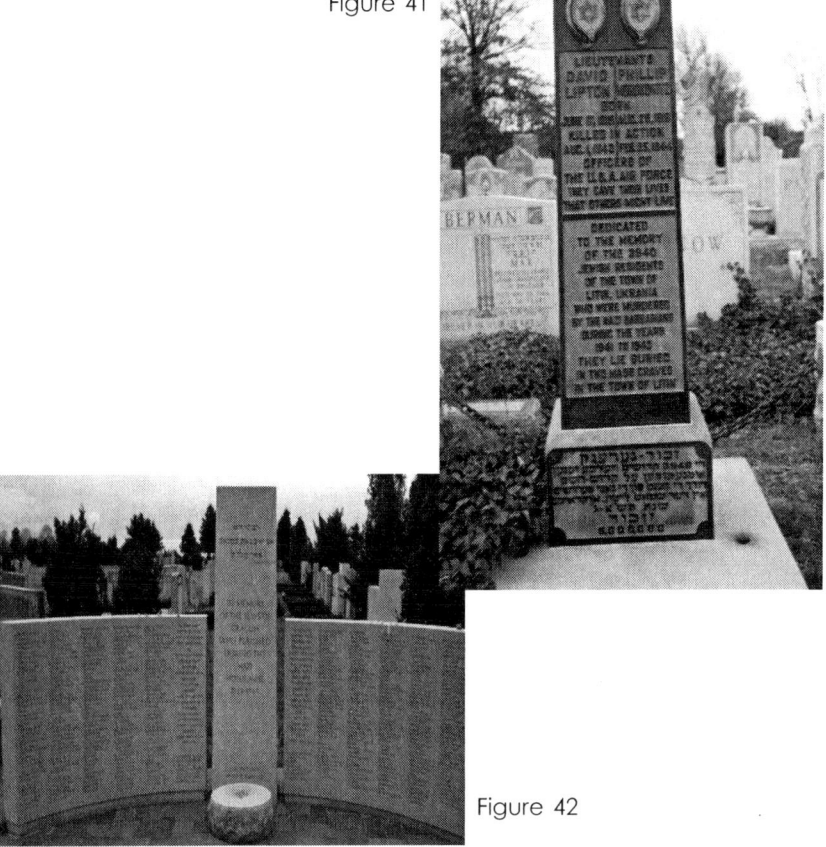

Figure 41

Figure 42

that were erected so soon after the Holocaust came to an end. Second, it lists the number of marytrs, 3,940, and states that they were buried in two mass graves. Third, it is one of the few memorials considered in this study that proclaims the number six million. Fourth, it also memorializes sons of organization members who lost their lives in the service as United States soldiers, as follows: "Lieutenants David Lipton and Phillip Mordkowitz, Officers of the United States of America Air Force – they gave their lives that others may live" (Figure 41).

The text declaring that the 3,940 martyrs were buried in two mass graves is given in English, but not in the Yiddish, which reads:

"Zochor-*Gedenk*
Remember
Dee 3,940 k'doshim velche zenen umgekumen al kiddush ha-Shem
The 3,940 holy martyrs who were murdered for the Sanctification of God's Name
durch dee hent fun dee Nazi merders
at the hands of the Nazi killers
in der shtot Litin
in the town of Litin, 1941–43. Yizkor, Remember, six million."

Names of martyrs are listed on the back of the monument.

Among the most attractive of the memorials studied is that erected at Beth Moses Cemetery by the New Cracow Friendship Society (Figure 42). It consists of one tall pillar flanked by two long and wide ones. The text, from Lamentations 1:12, is inscribed in Hebrew, with the source listed in English, and then a simple statement in English; "In Memory of the Jews of Cracow who perished during the Nazi Holocaust, 1939-1945."

This well-designed monument forms a gentle semi-circle, in the front of which is a small circular stone with a menorah.

It is located at the edge of the Society's plot, next to the street, and is therefore visible and noticeable. Names of the leaders of the Cracow Jewish community are listed in Hebrew; hundreds of others in English. The monument contains an added inscription: "Erected 1969 by their families."

CHAPTER FIVE
SELF-SACRIFICE OF ARTUR ZYGELBOIM

This Chapter deals not with organizations, as have all the foregoing, but with an individual. It is placed here for two compelling reasons. First, more than an organization, this individual represented the entire Jewish community of wartime Poland. Secondly, the monument to his memory is a memorial not to him alone, but equally to his colleagues who fought and died in the Warsaw Ghetto.

The person is Artur Shmuel Mordechai Zygelboim; the monument is located at New Mt. Carmel Cemetery in Ridgewood, New York. Zygelboim did not die in the United States, and therein lies a story of heroism and sacrifice.

Artur Zygelboim was a member of the Polish Government-in-Exile which found refuge in London after Hitler's invasion of Poland. Zygelboim had been one of the leaders of the Bund (Jewish labor movement), and was one of the few who escaped Poland after the invasion. He travelled from one non-occupied country to another, and reached London in 1942. As representative of the Jewish community in Poland, he saw his responsibility was to do everything possible to draw the attention of the world to the decimation of the Polish Jews by the Nazis.

In disappointment and anguish he saw that his efforts were not successful. When news reached him of the Warsaw Ghetto revolt, and how it was put down, he decided upon a personal act of protest against the callous attitude of the world toward what he saw as genocide being perpetrated by the Nazis. He committed suicide, leaving letters explaining his motives.

His ashes were brought to the United States and buried at New Mt. Carmel Cemetery. The monument over his grave is one of the most meaningful memorials of all in this study.

Figure 43

It is a beautiful monument. Because the marble is in a pink hue, it particularly stands out from adjacent monuments. Its hexagonal shape symbolizes the six million Jews whom he joined by his suicide. The monument, about five feet high, is surmounted by an eternal light formed by six tongues of flame, also representing the memory of the six million.

On the front of the monument is a statement of the position he held and the cryptic phrase: "Chose Martyr's death" (Figure 43).

The Yiddish is far more meaningful: *"Makriv geven zain leben far'n folk* – he sacrificed his life for the people." On the other panels are quotes in Yiddish and English translation from the letter he left behind.

"*Maineh chaverim in Varshaver Ghetto*
    my comrades in the Warsaw Ghetto
Zainen umgekumen mit gever een hant
    were killed with arms in their hands
een dem letzten heroishen gerangel
    in the last heroic battle.
Ess eez mir nisht geven bashert
    it was not ordained for me
tzu shtarben azoi vee zai, tzuzamen mit zai
    to die as they did, together with them
Ober ich geher tzu zai, und tzu zayer massen kvorim
    but I belong to them and to their common graves."
"*Mit mein toit vill ich oisdriken dem shtarksten protest*
    by my death I want to express my strongest protest
kegn dee passivkeit
    against the passivity
mit velcher dee velt kookt zich tzu
    with which the world watches
und derlozt
    and permits
dee ois-ratung fun yiddishen folk
    the extermination of the Jewish people." (Figure 44)

> "*Ich kohn nisht blaiben shtill, ich kohn nisht leben*
> I cannot remain quiet, I cannot go on living
> *ven dee reshtlech fun yiddishen folk een Poilen*
> when the remnants of the Jewish people in Poland
> *vemens forshtayer ich bin*
> whose representative I am
> *ver'n umgebracht*
> are being destroyed.
> "*Mein leben gehert tzum yiddishen folk een Poilen*
> my life belongs to the Jewish people in Poland
> *und derfar geeb ich ess eem avek*
> and therefore I give it back to them."

It is an unfortunate and sad fact that Zygelboim's suicide did not galvanize the free world into action. After the Warsaw Ghetto revolt, millions of Jews were yet to be destroyed, as the memorials in this study attest so eloquently (Figure 44).

Regretably, the Zygelboim monument, so important to the history of the Holocaust, will be little seen. First, it is located in a cemetery hardly used (New Mt. Carmel, Queens, NY), and not easily found. Second, even within this cemetery, the monument's location is in a section furthest from the entrance, and thus very difficult to locate. A great pity.

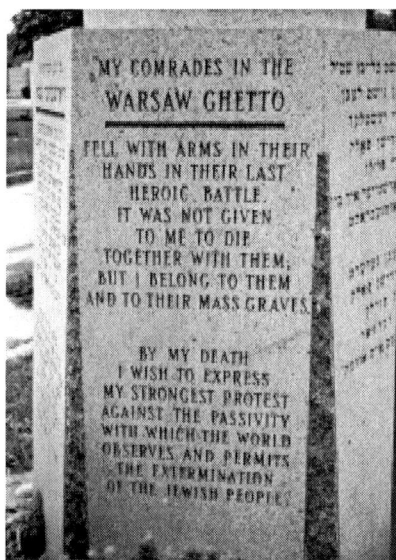

Figure 44

CHAPTER SIX
MID-SIZED MEMORIALS

The group of monuments described in this chapter are of medium size with limited texts inscribed upon them. In Mt. Hebron Cemetery is located the memorial erected by the Dombrover Society (Figure 45). The text is completely in Hebrew and principally mourns the foremost personality of the town, its Rabbi.

> "*Matzevas Zikaron*
>   a monument of Remembrance
> *l'hanoch k'doshim anoshim noshim v'tof*
>   to these holy martyrs – men, women and children
> *m'kehillah ha-k'doshah Dombrova v'ha-seviva*
>   from the holy community of Dombrov and environs
> *u-v'roshom ho-av-bais-din, raboh shel ho-ir*
>   and, chief among them, the head of the Court of Law,
>   the Rabbi of the city
> *ha-gaon mi-b'nay elyon ha-mu-otim*
>   the preeminent scholar who was from among the few
>   spiritual leaders of great distinction
> *morenu ha-rav Reb Nochum Weidenfeld*
>   our master Rabbi Nochum Weidenfeld
> *v' zugoso u-mish-pachto*
>   his wife and family
> *she-ne-hergu al kiddush Ha-Shem*
>   who were killed for the Sanctification of God's Name
> *al y'day ha-Natzim yimach sh'mom b'shnas tof-shin-hay*
>   at the hands of the Nazis – may their name be erased –
>   during the year 1945."

We note here an evident error in the text obviously made by the monument maker. The second word on the fourth line is inscribed האג"ד when it without doubt should have been האב"ד, which

Figure 45

Figure 46

stands for *ho-av-bais-din,* a famous acronym, meaning head of the rabbinical court. It seems evident that the workman mistook the ב for a ג. The rest of the space on this monument, front and back, is given over to a list of names of the martyrs from this community.

Also on Mt. Hebron Cemetery is the marker erected by the Independent Chodorower Young Men's Benevolent Society (Figure 46). It is our first example of the use of the gates of the Society's plot to memorialize the martyrs of the Holocaust. The existence of gates on cemetery grounds is common. The use of them as memorials is not. Most often they are used to inscribe the names of Society officers and members of the Cemetery committee. Here both are inscribed – the officers and the memorial, with far more prominence given to the memorial. Then the text continues with a quotation from Jeremiah 8:23:

> "Mee yitain roshee mayim v'aynee m'kor deemoh v'evkeh yomom vo'lailoh es challelay bas ami."
> "Oh that there be within me water enough that I may weep day and night and in my eyes tears enough to mourn the fallen of my people . . ." (Figure 46)

First, we find an expressive heading: "L'zichron olami – For an eternal remembrance."

The Yiddish text provides a reference not found in the English version; and vice versa. The former cites the six million martyrs, one of the few memorials in the study which refers explicitly to this number.

In the English version only the numer of martyrs from their home town, Chodorow, is mentioned: "The 1700 men, women and children of Chodorow, slain at the brutal hands of the Nazi invaders.:

> "*Tzum eibiken ondenk*
>   in eternal memory
> *fun dee zex million k'doshim b'chlall*
>   of the six million holy martyrs in sum
> *und bazunder fun dee Chodorover k'doshirn und martyer*
>   and especially of the holy martyrs from Chodorow
> *umgebracht gevoren fun dee Nazi rotzchim*
>   killed by the Nazi murderers
> *b'ays der tzvaiter velt milcho-moh*
>   during the Second World War 1941-1943."

The monument erected by the Ladies Auxiliary of the Stoliner Center in 1963 at the Beth David Cemetery memorializes their relatives from Stolin who perished in 1942, and lists almost fifty families with many more names.

The United Tarnopol Relief Society also erected a monument at Beth David Cemetery which laments the destruction of Jewish life and

Figure 47

Figure 48

culture in their home town.

Like the Chodorower Society the gate of the cemetery plot of the Nova Ushitza Society (Figure 47) is specifically dedicated to the memory of the martyrs, according to the text of the inscription at Beth David Cemetery:

> "*Ha-geder shel bais almin zeh*
>   the gate of this cemetery
> *mukdash l'zaicher ha-k'doshim may-ir nova ushitza*
>   is dedicated to the memory of the holy martyrs from the
>   town Nova Ushitza
> *she-mosru es nafshom al k'dushas Ha-She*m
>   who gave up their lives for the Sanctification of
>   God's Name
> *may-ha-natzim ha-t'mayim*
>   at the hands of the foul Nazis
> *u-vee-la ha-movess lo-netzach*
>   and may death disappear forever
> *v'yo-kutzu kol shoch-nay ofor*
>   and may all those who slumber in the dust awaken."

The Zinkov Society of the United States and Canada erected a monument at Old Montefiore Cemetery (Figure 48) which contains a most meaningful text in Hebrew and Yiddish. It is in the form of verse:

> "*K'doshaynu she-ne-esfu ba-shoah--al tishkach*
>   Our holy martyrs who perished in the Holocaust,
>   do not forget
> *Domom she-nish-pach b'retzach-al tachmol*
>   Their blood which was spilled murderously,
>   do not forgive!"

A Yiddish text follows, also in verse:

> "*Far dee letzte fun an eidoh, a zaicher*
>   For the remainder of a community, a remembrance
> *Zeier umshuldigen unkum, l'doros a dermanung*
>   Their innocent destruction, for generations a reminder.
>   May their souls rest in peace."

On the grounds of the Ostrover Sick Benevolent Society a

monument to their martyrs was erected by a member, Saul Rosen, to immortalize the memory of his wife, Miriam. This is an unusual departure from the norm; it is the only memorial to a Society's martyr erected by a private individual.

The text speaks of the desecration of the cemetery in Ostrove, as well as of the martyrs who perished in the gas chambers. The monument was presented in 1959.

Congregation B'nei Isaac Anshei Narajow has erected a monument at Beth David Cemetery that bears a simple three line text, the names of the donors and over sixty family names.

A unique monument in appearance, text and purpose was erected by the Globoker Surivors in America in 1980. Here, an American society memorializes its own members, rather than family in Europe. This group of Holocaust survivors from the same town of Globoke, dedicated this memorial to the events they themselves had lived through. It is truly one of its kind.

Fashioned of black marble it features an illustration of a fire with the flames burning three logs. (Figure 49) Above the flame is the word *Yizkor. Remember!* Each log represents the date of a massacre: 9 Nisan 1942, 4 Tammuz 1942 and 19 Av 1943.

The text, only in English, is a dedication to martyrs and also to the fighters – one of the few which mentions the resistance. "Dedicated to all who perished in the three massacres in the Ghetto Globoke, Poland, and in tribute to the partisans who died fighting the Nazis in the forests during the Holocaust of World War II."

This monument is particularly salient because it is an eternal memorial by those who actually lived through the experiences described thereon. It also relates a tale of resistance to the Nazis not told on any other monument in our study, namely, the fighting by the partisans. In this respect it is unique.

Figure 49

The Piltzer Benevolent Association has erected a monument at Wellwood Cemetery the text of which contains a significant phrase in Hebrew:

> "*Zeechrom shel ha-k'doshim shomur v'roshum al luach leebo shel amaynu lo-netzach*
> the memory of our holy martyrs will be protected and etched upon the chambers of the hearts of our people forever."

The English text expresses the hope that the martyrs will "never be forgotten by mankind." The monument also contains a listing of families who were put to death in the years of the Holocaust.

On the grounds of the Kossover Society at New Montefiore Cemetery a monument was erected especially in memory of their family members who were killed in the gas chambers of Treblinka. The text is in both the Hebrew and English. (Figure 50)

One phrase in English is particularly poignant: "so that others may live." That phrase was also used on the monument of the Litiner Society in reference to members' sons who were killed in action while serving in the United States armed forces. Of course, whether the martyrs went to their death in the gas chambers and crematoria "so that

Figure 50　　　　　　　　　Figure 51

others may live" is an open question.

The Plancher Benevolent Society's memorial monument at New Montefiore Cemetery is noteworthy because it establishes the *yom ha-zikoron,* the Day of Remembrance *(Yahrzeit)* as 6 Cheshvan 1943, and explicitly refers to the Nazis as "beasts" (Figure 51). It was erected in 1967.

Two other monuments of note are to be found at Baron de Hirsch cemetery in Staten Island. They are located less than a block away from each other, and one is a replica of the other. (Figure 52) One was dedicated by the Zdunska-Wola Society in 1954, and the other by the Poloner Independent Aid Society just ten years later, in 1964. Both have very short texts, the Zdunska monument in Yiddish, English and Hebrew, while the Poloner is in Yiddish and English only.

Another monument in the Baron de Hirsch cemetery is of interest because it relies on a picture rather than words to relate its story. It was erected in memory of the victims of Skarzysko (Figures 53 and 54). Etched into the granite is the portrayal of a Jewish family in Poland, as evidenced by their style of clothing, standing in the ruins of a destroyed house, with flames still rising on either side. It is a heart-rending scene of children embracing parents – son, father, daughter, mother – in a last tearful farewell. It is a poignant depiction of ruined life and torn families. The inscription above in English, says only: "In memory of our beloved in the town of Skarzysko, 1939-1945." The pillar is surmounted by an eternal light in the form of a flame.

It should be pointed out that there are only two other monuments that have this kind of etching, the Disner Society (Figures 62 and 63) and the Jarowower Society (Figure 55). Neither compares in scope and detail with the Skarzyko memorial. The Jarowower monument merely shows a Jew in a *tallis,* while the Disner is more comprehensive – a village on a slope with an ascending sun in the horizon. In contrast, the Skarzysko memorial, is extremely original.

Yiddish Mayden martyrs were slaughtered on the day of Yom Kippur 1943, according to the memorial erected on Beth David Cemetery by their *landsleit.* As with the Chodorower and Nova Ushitza societies, the text is inscribed in Hebrew and in English on either post

Figure 52

Figure 53

of the entrance to the Society's plot (Figure 56).

The Lanzut Belevolent Association has erected a memorial to their relatives from that town. It is located at Mt. Judah Cemetery in Ridgewood, NY. It bids for our attention because the Hebrew text is almost profuse in its detail:

> "In eternal memory of the holy martyrs of Lanzut
> *she-huglu, nis-r'fu, v'hush-m'du*
> who were exiled, burned and destroyed
> *b'r'chovos ho'ir, b'ya-aros pulkini*
> in the streets of the town, in the forests of Polkini, Belziz and Milnik
> *uv'darchay n'duday-hem*
> and on the many roads of their wanderings

> *al y'day ha-tzor'rim ha'germanim, u-g'rurayhem,*
> *yimach sh'mom –*
> at the hands of the persecutors, the Germans and their partners, may their names be erased."

> *"Zichrom ha-kodosh lo yomush mee-keerbaynu*
> Their holy memory shall never be removed from within us
> *u-mee-layv ah-maynu ad sof ha-doros*
> and from the hearts of our nation until the end of time."

The day of remembrance, *Yahrzeit,* is proclaimed as 21 Av. Once again we find a moving memorial inscription in Hebrew which is inadequately translated into English.

A more evenly translated inscription from the Hebrew to the English is a companion memorial on Mt. Judah Cemetery. It is that of the Serheier Society. The Yiddish deserves to be heard:

> *"mir velen aiyer far-peinigten toit kaynmohl nit fargesen*
> your tortured death we will never forget
> *und aiyer peiniger aibig gedenken*
> and your torturers we will always remember."

Date of massacre is listed as September 20, 1941.

All of the memorials discussed so far were erected in memory of European Jewish communities, *Ashkenazim,* as they are popularly called. For the first and only time in this study, we now encounter a Holocaust memorial for Jews who are *Sephardim*. This monument was erected by the Rhodes League of Brothers at Beth Israel Cemetery, in Woodbridge, New Jersey, and memorializes Jews from the Isle of Rhodes who were victims of the Holocaust (Figure 57). Perusing this list of names makes it abundantly clear that the Jews of central Europe were not the only victims of the Nazi policy of "final solution." Alhadeff, Benveniste, Mizrahi, Rousso, Turiel and others were equally martyrs *"al kiddush Ha-Shem* – for the Sanctification of God's Name."

Also on Beth Israel Cemetery is the monument of the Chmielnik Society, which vows "we will never forget or forgive." It is set

Figure 54

Figure 55

Figure 56

apart with posts and chain surrounding it. There is a text in English on the front, and in Hebrew and Yiddish on the back. (Figure 58)

The Grodzisker Mutual Aid Society monument at United Hebrew Cemetery memorializes five thousand men, women and children slain by the Nazis between 1939 and 1945. Psalm 79:10 is quoted in Hebrew and English. It comes from the liturgy of the Sabbath service and is a dirge to the martyrs:

> *"Yee-voda ba-goyim l'ay-naynu nikmas dam a-vo-decho ha-shofuch*
> May the avenging of Thy servants spilt blood be made known among the nations, witnessed by us."

Names of victims fill the back and two sides. (Figure 59)

Another of the earliest monuments, erected in 1949 by the Solotwiner Sick and Benevolent Society, is found at Mt. Hebron Cemetery. Here again we find a distinction between the text in the Hebrew and that of the English. The Hebrew begins with a prayer of *Yizkor* for the souls of brothers from Solotwina who perished, and then mentions *"v'ess nishmas b'nay-nu she-noflu b'mil-chemess ho-olom* – and the souls of our sons who fell in World War II." (Figure 60)

The English version speaks first of "its member's Sons who sacrificed their lives on the altar of democracy," and, secondly, refers to the "beloved martyred kinsmen of Solotwina." We seek but do not find an explanation for this order of selection.

Figure 57

Figure 58

Figure 59

Figure 60

CHAPTER SEVEN
SMALL MEMORIALS WITH SPECIFIC TEXT

The Old Sinover Society and Ladies Auxiliary has erected a small monument with a large message. It is located at Mt. Hebron Cemetery and contains a short text in Hebrew and English. This proves to be one of the most arresting of inscriptions because of its Biblical reference.

As has previously been noted, there are any number of quotations from Scriptures on monuments. This is the only one in the study, however, which paraphrases the Biblical verse, and refers to the Nazis in the language of the Bible.

Figure 61

The Hebrew text is: *"Zochor ess asher osoh l'cho Amalek ha-Nazi."* It is accurately translated as: "Remember what was done to you by Amalek the Nazi" (Figure 61).

In the Biblical idiom, Amalek is put in the role of the archenemy of the Jews. This stems from the account in Exodus 17:8-16 and repeated in Deuteronomy 25:17-19 which describes an unprovoked attack by the ancient people Amalek against the Israelites. In the latter reference the Bible mentions that the attack was made upon the defenseless and weary stragglers. From that time on, Amalek was a term of opprobrium by which Israel's enemies were known. The primary example of this is Haman, the anti-Semite of the Book of Esther who was, according to tradition, a descendant of the

Amalekites.

The Bible adds the admonition to Israel: *"Zochor, al tishkach!* Remember, do not forget!" Hence, parenthetically, Shabbos *Zochor,* the Sabbath of Remembrance, is assigned for the Sabbath before Purim, and the reading from the Torah is this section of the Bible, referring to the hateful attack upon the defenseless. The command of the Almighty was to "blot out" the remembrance of a people (the Amalekites) who possessed no native feelings of pity and no natural qualities of humanity.

The text of this monument shouts out in loud terms that the Nazis who perpetrated the inhumanities of the Holocaust were the heirs of the Amalekites of old.

This is further expressed by the added inscription on the face of the Sinover monument:

> *"Am yisroel*
>   the People of Israel
> *ess k'doshov she-nehergu, nish-ch'tu v'nis-r'fu*
>   its holy martyrs who were killed, slaughtered and burned
> *al kiddush ha-Shem*
>   for the Sanctification of the Name of God
> *v'kiddush ho-om*
>   and their sacred devotion to the People of Israel."

Parenthetically, and it is almost irreverent to point it out, there is a small but glaring error in the Hebrew text: the first word of the second line, "asher," is spelled with an "ayin" instead of an "aleph." (Figure 62)

The stinging message of this monument will fall mostly upon deaf ears, since as mentioned earlier, the declaration that the Jewish People was decimated by the hated enemy is in Hebrew. The English version bids the beholder: "Remember what was done to you by Amalek the Nazi." One unfamiliar with the Bible and with the connection between Amalek and anti-Semitism will lose the symbolism intended. Alas!

A number of reasons make the monument erected in 1964 by the Disner Benevolent Association at Old Montefiore Cemetery noteworthy. First, it specifically identifies the date of destruction: June 15, 1942. Thus it establishes a *Yahrzeit:* 2 Tammuz. Second, it is one of only three in the entire study which bears an illustration (the other two are the Skarzysker and the Jawaworer). This sketch, on the bottom of one side of the column, depicts a small cluster of houses resting upon the slope of a hill. The houses are low with flat roofs. Several domes are visible. Some of the trees appear to be palms. This scene seems to be set in Israel. A road winds through the town, leading upward into a rising sun, possibly suggesting hope for the dawn of a new day in the Homeland? (Figure 62) Third, the Yiddish is again very vivid as contrasted with the English. The English version speaks of "the martyrs of Disner exterminated by the Nazi murderers." In Yiddish we read:

>"*dee tei-eh-reh fun unser hailiker kehilla Disna*
>   our beloved from our holy community of Disna
>*vos zenen ois-ge-harget, farbrent*
>   who were exterminated, burned
>*un lebediker-hayt ba-groben gevoren*
>   and buried alive
>*durch dee merderliche Nazis*
>   at the hands of the murderous Nazis
>*Zayer hailiker ondenk vet zain mit uns aibik*
>   their sacred memory will be with us always." (Figure 63)

On the same street in an adjoining plot is the monument of the Mariampol Society. It quotes the dirge from the Book of Lamentations 1:12, that we have seen on a number of other monuments: "Behold and see if there be any sorrow like my sorrow." It also specifies a date on which the massacre took place, Yom Kippur, 1941. (Figures 64 and 64A)

Two monuments at Beth David Cemetery are similar insofar as their text is only in Hebrew. No English translation. The Trisk-Volin Society (Figure 65) speaks of

>"*horaynu, achaynu, v'achyosaynu*
>   our parents, our brothers, our sisters
>*ha-ne-ehovim, v'ha-n 'eemeem*
>   the beloved, the sweet
>*y'leeday Trisk-Volin*
>   born in our town

Figure 62

Figure 63

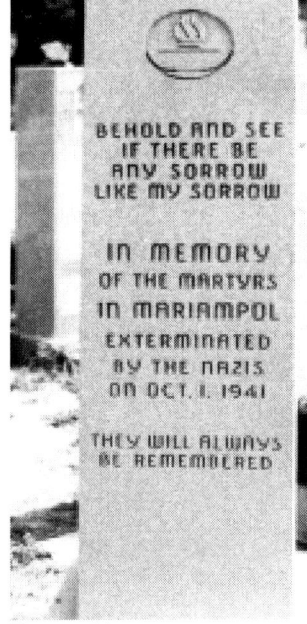

BEHOLD AND SEE
IF THERE BE
ANY SORROW
LIKE MY SORROW

IN MEMORY
OF THE MARTYRS
IN MARIAMPOL
EXTERMINATED
BY THE NAZIS
ON OCT. 1, 1941

THEY WILL ALWAYS
BE REMEMBERED

Figure 64

Figure 64A

Figure 65

Figure 66

Figure 67

Figure 68

>   *she-nirtz'chu v'nisr'fu*
>   who were murdered and burned
>   *bee-y'day ha-zaydim ha-Germanim ha-Natzim, yimach shmom*
>   at the hands of the villainous German Nazis, may their memories be erased – on the 12th of Elul, 1942."

On this monument we find two words *"ha-ne-ehovim v' ha-n eemeem,"* which are taken from the dirge for martyrs that is part of the Sabbath service. On the side of this monument, under the heading *"sh'mos ha-k'doshim* – names of the holy" is a listing of martyrs. (Figure 66)

The other monument which contains only a Hebrew text is that of the Malater Benevolent Society (Figure 67). It begins with the familiar quotation from Lamentations 1:16 – *"al aileh onu bochim* – for these do we weep – *v'aynaynu tay-radno d'moh-os* – and our eyes drip tears . . . for the holy and pure who were killed for the Sanctification of God's Name at the hands of the cursed Nazis."

Passersby who cannot read and understand Hebrew will never know what heinous tragedy these monuments commemorate!

It has previously been pointed out that it is a rather common practice for a gate to be erected at the entrance to a Society's cemetery grounds. These are customarily in the form of two standing columns on either side of the entrance. On those columns we usually find inscribed the names of the officers of the Society and/or those of the Cemetery Committee. Some memorials to the Holocaust have been placed on one or the other of such columns, either separately or as an addition to some existing text.

Figure 69

Such a design may be found on the gate to the grounds of the Burstyner Chevre Linas Hazedek at the Wellwood Cemetery in Pinelawn, LI, whose unique text chiefly commemorates graves in the home town which have been destroyed. It contains this significant inscription, in both Hebrew and English:

> "*Matzaivoh zu huk-moh*
> This monument has been erected
> *l'zichron y'huday eer Burstyn*
> in memory of the Jews of the town of Burstyn
> *she-maysu v 'nik-beru b'vais ha-chayim d'hosom*
> who died and were buried in the Jewish cemetery there
> *v'al gabay kivrosayhem chorshu ha-choshrim*
> and over their graves the ploughers plowed."
> (Figure 68)

Evidently, the members of this Society were more concerned with the destruction of the old Cemetery and the grave markers there than they were of the martyrs of the Holocaust, for the latter is added almost as if an afterthought. Indeed, in the Hebrew the victims of the Holocaust are not even mentioned, although they are in the English: "This monument is to commemorate all those Jewish graves which are no longer marked in Burstyn, and to those who were killed in the Holocaust 1941-1945."

Another gatepost dedication seems to have been sponsored by three families, independent of the organization. The names of these sponsors are listed on the bottom of the post. The top bears the word "*Yizkor* – May God Remember," followed by a brief text: "*Lizkor Olom,*" which is an obvious error. It should read either "*L'zaycher olom* – an eternal remembrance (without the '*vov*')," or else "*Lizkor l'olom* – to remember forever (with the addition of a '*lamed*' to the beginning of the second word).

> "*L-han-tzee-ach achaynu ha-k'doshim may-eeraynu ha-y'karoh Shebreshin*
> to eternalize our holy brethren from our beloved town Shebreshin
> *she-nirts'chu b'lee rach-monus al y'day ach- zorim –*
> who were murdered without mercy by the cruel ones."
> (Figure 69)

The English text contains two interesting sidelights. It refers to the "enshrined city" of Shebreshin, and concludes "Shebreshiner posterity lives on."

The Hrubieshow Sick Benevolent Society monument at New

Figure 70

Figure 71

Figure 71A

Figure 72

Montefiore Cemetery is the only monument in the study which actually mentions Hitler. The English version of the text reads: "In memory of our people of Hrubieshow whose lives were wantonly and mercilessly cut short by the Nazi Hitler regime." (Figure 70) The Hebrew version speaks of the *"Nazis und zay-ereh arois helfers* – the Nazis and those who assisted them" which is a reference we have not found too often in this study.

We next encounter a small monument whose text is entirely in Hebrew. It was erected by the Skidel Society at Beth Israel Cemetery. It contains two sentences from the dirge for the martyrs in the Sabbath service: *"Av Ho-racha-mim* – Father of Mercy." The first is *"Ha-ne-ehovim v'ha-n'eemeem b'cha-yayhem* – they were beloved and pleasant in their lifetime – *uv'mosom lo nifrodu*—and in death they were not separated." And it ends with a paraphrase of a second, *"v'yinkom l'aynanu nikmas dam avodecho ha-shofuch* – and may the Almighty render retribution in our time for the wantonly spilt blood of Thy servants."

Another set of cemetery gateposts is inscribed in verse as a memorial to the victims of the families of the First Jaworower Independent Society at Beth Moses Cemetery. The etching here is the form of an elder wrapped in a *tallis,* reading from a scroll. The Hebrew poem is written in starker terms than those rendered in the English on the opposite post.

"*L'zaycher olom*
    In eternal remembrance
L'ir nech-modoh Yavorov
    to the beautiful town of Yaworow
she-tov'u bo-oretz she-oreho
    whose gates were sunk into the earth
she-hutzas aish boh va-yaver rav
    which was set on fire and burned so many
va-taychel boh es kol ha-moneho.
    and all its population was destroyed.
Boh ovar sh'ays v'hashber
    Within it took place ravage and destruction
she-yotz'oh may-am b'nay bli-ah-yal
    which was the handiwork of the villains
ess nikmas dahm b'nay say-vehr
    the retribution of the blood of the children of hope

od yidrosh Eloha mee-mah-al
   will yet be demanded by God on High."
(Figures 71 and 71A)

This chapter concludes noting a small monument with a short text (Figure 72). It is one of the oldest, having been erected at Mt. Hebron Cemetery in 1951 by Narevker Society. It contains the word, *tal-yo-neem,* in the Hebrew text not found anywhere else in any of the other inscriptions recorded: "*dee Nazi tal-yo-neem* – the Natzi hangmen." Note, too, the misspelling *natzi.*

CHAPTER EIGHT
SMALL MEMORIALS WITH GENERAL TEXT

We now turn to a group of monuments with inscriptions that are general in nature. Some speak of *Kiddush HaShem,* some speak of Nazi tyranny, some offer a date of martyrdom, some are almost anonymous. All of them, however, have this in common – they refer to their own kin, members of their own families in the towns in which they originally lived and who perished during the Holocaust.

The Isbitze Society memorial in Old Montefiore Cemetery is the only one of this group that lists some martyrs (Figure 73). It is included here because of the generality of the text:

Figure 73

"*L'zaicher olom*
    In eternal remembrance
nishmos anshay Izbitze
    the souls of the people of Isbitze
she-nehergu, v'nish-ch'tu, v'nis-refu al kiddush ha-Shem b'shnas 1942
    who were killed, slaughtered and burned for the Sanctification of God's Name in 1942."

The First Titchiner Sick and Benevolent Society at Beth David Cemetery says: "*In dem ondenk fun dee Titchiner landsleit um-ge-kumen oif Kidush HaShem durch die Natzishe hent*"

It is fairly accurately translated beneath the Yiddish: "In memory of our Titchiner *landsleit* who died as a result of the Nazi persecutions in World War II." (Figure 74)

Figure 74

Figure 75

The Zezmer Society, also at Beth David Cemetery, memorializes in English only the "brothers and sisters and all our relatives in our town of Zezmer, Lithuania, who met a savage death at the hands of the Nazis during the destruction of the town."

Another monument at Beth David Cemetery, erected by the Lokatcher Society refers only to Lokatcher martyrs in Yiddish and English. However, on a slab which would serve as a cover for a grave there are two inscriptions in Hebrew. The first is a quotation from Scripture: Lamentations 5:17. *"Al zeh hoyoh doveh leebaynu, al ayleh chosh-chu aynaynu* — For this our heart has become faint, for these things our eyes have grown dim."

The second is the stark statement: *"Noflu al kdushas ha-Shem* — Martyred for the Sanctification of God's Name, 27 Elul-September 9, 1942."

The memorial established by the Zloczower Sick and Benevolent Association at Wellwood Cemetery is evidently an addition to the entrance gate previously erected. The gate posts themselves are filled with names of officers and members of the Society. To the left of this gate is a small free standing marker which contains the simple legend in English: "In memory of our brothers and sisters who were killed by the Nazis in our city Zloczow." (Figure 75)

The Baryszer Young Men's Benevolent Association, just across the street, also has utilized the gate posts for a memorial to the martyrs of their town. It is far more expressive in the Hebrew version:

Figure 76

Figure 77

Figure 78

Figure 79

> "*Chanun habitoh meem-romim*
> All Merciful, look down from the heavens
> *tash-pochess dahm ha-tzadikim*
> the spilt blood of the righteous
> *she-nehergu v'she-nish-chetu al kiddush ha-Shem*
> who were killed and slaughtered for the Sanctification of God's Name
> *bee-y'day ha-Natzim ho-r'shoyim*
> at the hands of the wicked Nazis
> *b'ir Barysz v'ha-s'vivos*
> in the town of Barysz and environs."

The abbreviation, *"tof, nun, tzadi, beis, hay,"* which follows, are the first letters of the Hebrew memorial phrase: *"T'hay naf shom tzruroh b'tzror ha-chayim* – May their souls be bound up in the bond of eternal life." (Figure 76)

It seems rather strange that this memorable phrase does not occur more often on the monuments in our study. It is a very popular text on monuments in general and is used on the overwhelming majority. The phrase *"Hashem Yinkom Domom* – May the Almighty avenge their blood" is found far more often. Perhaps in the minds of those who arranged the memorials, the latter phrase superseded the former in the circumstances being recorded.

Congregation Anshe Lebedowe and Radzilowe seems to have recorded the least specific of all the inscriptions we have found: "To our martyred brethren forever in our hearts 1933-1945." It would appear from the dates listed that the recorder failed to examine records when their towns came under the heel of the persecutors. Poland was not invaded until 1939 (Figure 77).

Chevra M'vak-shay Sholom Anshei Molodetshne erected a simple memorial at New Montefiore Cemetery which remembers "our relatives and *landsleit*. . .who were persecuted and slain by the Nazis during World War II." (Figure 78)

The Pomorzaner Society at Beth Moses Cemetery has inscribed a gate post in Hebrew only, beginning with the words of the traditional memorial prayer *"Yizkor Elohim es* – May God Remember– *horaynu u-krovaynu* – our parents and our relatives – *y'leeday ir* –natives of Pomorzaneh – she'nirtz-chu, v'nisrefu b'y-dai ha-Nazim, Yimach sh'mom – who were slaughtered and cremated by the Nazis – May the

Almighty avenge their blood." There follows the names of the martyred. Here, again, one who does not read Hebrew would have no idea who is being memorialized, or why (Figure 79).

This chapter concludes with another simple text on the gate post of Wladower Society at New Montefiore Cemetery. The side bears this legend, in English only: "In memory of our Martyrs of Nazi Persecution."

CHAPTER NINE
ORGANIZATION MONUMENTS WHICH ESTABLISH A DATE OF YAHRZEIT

In this study we have encountered many inscriptions which carry a date of a particular massacre. Some have more than one date. Most of the monuments in this study, however, do not carry a date of death. The obvious reason is that such a date is unknown to the survivors. In most cases, the martyrs perished at different times in different places. Seldom did information become available that the residents of a certain town or community were massacred on a specific day.

In this context two organizations are particularly noteworthy. They have erected rather large memorials to their martyrs, and although they did not know when they were killed, each group has established a date on its monument to be observed as a day of *Yahrzeit*.

Coincidentally, these monuments stand only a block away from each other at the same cemetery, Mt. Hebron. The first is the Bukaczowzer Society memorial, whose inscription is in both Yiddish and English. Under the Hebrew words: *"L'zaycher Olom* – In eternal remembrance," we read the following text:

> "*Tzum ondenk fun dee Bukachovtzer k'doshim un umgegung*
> In memory of the Bukachovtzer martyrs and environs – *umgekumen al kiddush ha-Shem een der tzvaiter velt milchomoh* – perished in the sanctification of God's name in World War II – *ha Shem yikom domom*
>   may the Almighty avenge their blood – may their souls rest in peace."

There follows a statement in Yiddish only: *"Mir hoben ba-shtimt zayer Yahrzeit Yom Kippur* – we have established their Yahrzeit Yom Kippur." The English legend which follows does not mention *Yahrzeit.* (Figure 80)

The Wishnewitz-Volyn Society has also erected a substantial memorial with a text in Hebrew and English. Under the heading *"L'zaycher olom* – In eternal remembrance" the following is inscribed:

> *"Matzevas Zikoron zeh l'k'doshay ir Wishnewitz-Volyn*
>   This memorial monument is for the martyrs of
>   Wishnewitz Volyn
> *she-nehergu al kiddush ha-Shem*
>   who were killed for the sanctification of God's Name
> *al y'day ha-Natzim v'ukrainim, yimach shmom*
>   at the hands of the Nazis and the Ukrainians, may their
>   names be erased
> *be-y'may ha'shoah v'ha-za-am b'shnass 1943*
>   during the days of the destruction and ravage in the
>   year 1943
> *yinkom ha'Shem ess domom ha-shofuch*
>   may the Almighty avenge their spilt blood."

Figure 80

Figure 81

The inscription concludes with the Hebrew and English: *"Yom ha-Yahrzeit nikba l'erev Rosh Hashonoh* – the Day of Yahrzeit is set for the eve of Rosh Hashonoh." (Figure 81)

This monument is particularly instructive to the American Jewish generation of the post-Holocaust era. It shows how an organization not only commemorates the martyrdom of its native sons and daughters, but proclaims a day of remembrance to be observed by their relatives and families. The monument thus becomes more than physical reminder – it also serves as a spiritual reminder as well to keep alive the memories of the martyrs year after year.

CHAPTER TEN
FAMILY MARKERS WITH MEMORIALS TO HOLOCAUST MARTYRS

The overwhelming majority of monuments to martyrs of the Holocaust had been erected by organizations whose members originated in the same town in Europe. But not all of them. A number of monuments were found that were intended primarily as memorials for the individuals who were interred in these metropolitan New York cemeteries, but the families also added the names of loved ones who perished in the Holocaust. And there were a few monuments dedicated to individual victims of the Holocaust. All these will be treated in this chapter.

We begin with a large family plot at the Old Montefiore Cemetery which was established for the descendants of one Pesach Notte. At the right of the entrance gate is a monument, larger than the rest, dedicated to members of this family who were victims of the Holocaust.

The Hebrew text is meaningful:

"*L'zichron netzach*
    In eternal remembrance
ha-k'doshim yotzay chalotzay Pesach Notte, zichrono l'vrocho
    of the martyrs who were descendants of Pesach Notte, of blessed memory
asher noflu al'yday ha-rotzchim ho-ashkenazim
    who perished at the hands of the German murderers
u-vaynayhem hoyu ayleh
    and among them were these:" (followed by names).

On the bottom is this text in English: "This marks the symbolic grave of all Pesach Notte descendants who were massacred by the Nazis and their ilk during World War II." (Figure 82)

The next monument belongs in the group of family markers because it was presented by an individual in memory of his wife, although it was actually dedicated to the Holocaust survivors of a certain town. Rose Holtzman is the deceased, and her husband presented the monument in her memory. The natives of Lipno are the ones

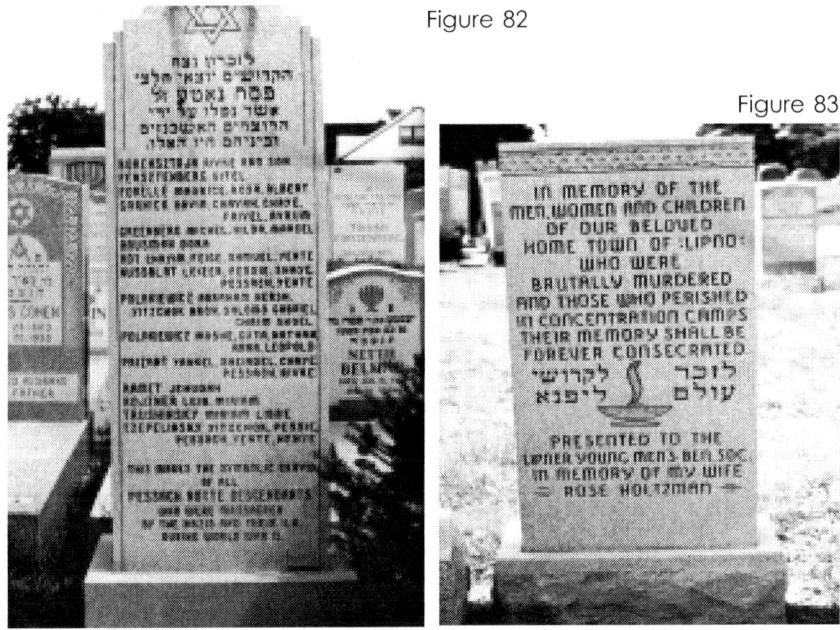

Figure 82

Figure 83

memorialized. The inscription is all in English with only four words in Hebrew: *"L'zaycher olom lee-k'doshay Lipno* – In eternal memory of the martyrs of Lipno." This monument is also in the Old Montefiore Cemetery (Figure 83).

At Baron de Hirsch Cemetery are three markers standing over empty graves! Each is a standard sized monument, erected in memory of members of a family that perished in the Holocaust. Their names are listed. The English relates the life and fate of the relatives.

On the first marker: "Schneiderman Family, who perished in the Holocaust. Rivka Faerstein Schneiderman, born 1886, Helm, Poland, Died 1943, Camp Cibiba, Poland." Others follow.

The final entry is of special interest. "Jacob Schneiderman, musician, born Helm, Poland, Died Fighting in the Warsaw Ghetto, 1940-1941."

The inscription on the bottom is an obvious paraphrase of the prayer in the Passover Haggadah: "Bless Him who brought us from darkness to great light."

> *"L'fichoch anachnu chayovim* –
>   therefore we are dutybound –
> *l'voraych* – to bless –
> *l'mee she-ho-tzee-onu may-afaylo l'or godol* –
>   Him who brought us from deep darkness to great light."

The second monument in this family group memorializes the Waksman Family and lists nine individuals, including a child, who died in the Holocaust. The text concludes with the English version of verse 4 in the 23rd Psalm, "I will fear no evil for Thou art with me."

The third marker in this group is an effort to memorialize other members of this family whose names are unknown. This inscription calls to mind a similar one – the Otynier Society memorial, which remembers all those "known only to God."

Another monument of this type stands upon the Balaban Family Plot at Beth David Cemetery. The text is only in English: "In memory of our beloved parents massacred in Europe in 1941," and their names, followed by the legend: "Erected by son-in-law and daughters," and "Erected by sons and daughter." Very few such markers are to be seen in the cemeteries in our study.

At the Beth David Cemetery is a private plot of the Hirschbaum-Goldbaum Family. An entrance gate has been erected. On the left post are names of the two families, while on the right post we find a memorial inscription to victims of the Holocaust. The text reads: "In memory of all those who perished in the Holocaust in Europe 1933-1945." (Figure 84)

Note the absence of any specific reference to family or relatives. It seems reasonable to assume that this memorial is an effort by a private family to memorialize the Holocaust in a simple, yet conclusively

Figure 84

Figure 85

Figure 86

Figure 87

appropriate manner. (It is an effort that should be commended and encouraged – for, in the opinion of the author, it heightens the consciousness of the beholder to the era of the Holocaust.)

There is a memorial in the Old Montefiore Cemetery that is not a monument. It is a bench on a family plot, erected by sisters in memory of their sister and her family *"gefalene korbonos fun dee brutaleh Nazis in Vinitze 1941* – martyred victims of the brutal Nazis in Vinitze 1941." It is written only in Yiddish (Figure 85).

We cturn now to a series of monuments that have been erected over standard grave sites, which bear an epitaph not only for the deceased, but includes additional text which memorializes members of the deceased's family who perished in the Holocaust.

At Beth David Cemetery is a monument for Mordechai Farkash (Figure 86), with this text in Hebrew:

"V'ho-even ha-zos ti-h'yeh gam l'zichron olom a'lee-yas nish-mas oveev v'eemo oh-cheev, v'ach-yoso
and this monument shall also be an everlasting remembrance for the ascent to Heaven of the souls of his father and his mother, his brother and his sisters"

and they are all named

"she-ne-hergu al kiddush ha-Shem b'shnos ha-za-am, ha-Shem yikom domom
who were killed for the Sanctification of God's Name during the Holocaust – May their death be avenged."

An additional brief caption specifies: *"Hamatzevah* ha-*zos he-emeedoh ayshes ha-niftar* – this monument was erected by the wife of the deceased," who is named, and their daughter and son-in-law, may they be granted life. It concludes: *"Y'hee maylitz tov avuram* – may the deceased be a good advocate for them."

At the New Montefiore Cemetery we see a monument for a survivor who came to these shores and remarried. He passed away and is buried on this plot, and his second wife survived him. The monument is a double stone, very common, and the inscription for the survivor is already on the stone, also rather common, awaiting only a date of death for completion of the text. Less common are the two added inscriptions memorializing relatives of each of them who died in the Holocaust.

On the bottom is an inscription in memory of the husband's first wife and children who did not survive.

"In memory of Avrohom Pesach's wife, Gitel Glezer Barish, and his three children, Esther, Berel, Matel – Died in the Holocaust at Auschwitz, January 1943." On the top is this text: "In Memory of Molly's parents, brothers and sisters, died in the Holocaust." (Figure 87)

As we have seen, choice of English for such an inscription is unusual. Most were exclusively in Hebrew.

At the Old Montefiore Cemetery, for example, a monument for Rabbi Yechezkel Deren carries this addition in Hebrew:

"*U-l'zaycher nishmas aviv ha-muflog b'Torah v'yir-ahs sho-mayim, she-ne-herag al kiddush ha-Shem*
and in memory of the soul of his father, outstanding in scholarship and reverence, who was killed for the Sanctification of God's Name
ho-Rav ha-Chosid Reb Yisrael ben Yechezkel Ha-Cohen
The Rabbi the Chasid Israel ben Ezekiel the Cohen –may his death be avenged."

Each of the next four monuments, all at New Montefiore Cemetery, is a

Figure 90

Figure 91

Figure 92

memorial to a person buried there, and to their respective inscriptions is added a remembrance of members of the immediate family perished in the Holocaust. All are in Hebrew. The first, for Rebitzin Lifshitz, is an elaborate legend, concluding with: *"L'zaycher nishmas ho-reho hak'doshim she-nehergu al kiddush ha-Shem* – in memory of her holy parents who were killed for the Sanctification of God's Name." Their names follow.

The second monument, for a 22-year-old student at the Lakewood, New Jersey Yeshiva who died in an accident, has a longer list of those who died in the Holocaust: the boy's grandparents on his father's side are named, his grandparents on his mother's side and the other members of the family killed *"b'ymay ha-Shoah* – in the era of the Holocaust."

The Kotner Family has added an inscription in memory of its members from Alexandrof, and names the father, mother, brothers and sisters killed in the Holocaust.

And on the monument for a venerable aged scholar, Avrohom Bergstein, there is added an inscription to memorialize his young son, Moshe Chaim, who was a student at the Yeshiva of Kletzk in Poland, "killed for the Sanctification of God's Name." (Figure 90) Perhaps this is a family which had already emigrated to America and whose son was sent back to the yeshiva in Europe because of its high standards for Talmudic scholarship. Was he caught and killed along with other Yeshiva students as the Nazis invaded Poland?

The two monuments which follow have inscriptions, in Yiddish, that tell us that the individuals were leaders in the Bund, the Jewish Socialist Party in Poland. The first, for Emanuel Nowogrodzki (Figure 91), also memorializes his wife who met death in Treblinka. The text describes her as *"'TZISHA,' lererin, Bundishe tu-erin, ahktive een varshaver ghetto, umgebracht in Treblinka* – 'TZISHA,' teacher, a worker for the Bund, active in the Warsaw Ghetto, was killed in Treblinka."

The second, for Mark Wasser, Chairman of the Central Committee of the Bund in Poland, memorializes his wife, Mania, and his daughter, Hanusha, killed by the Nazis in August, 1944. (Figure 92)

At the Adas Yereim grounds at the Beth Israel Cemetery are located a large number of monuments which bear inscriptions memorializing kin who perished in the Holocaust. The four which

Figure 91

Figure 92

follow are representative.

The first is a monument to one of the greatest Rabbinic authorities in the Orthodox world, Rabbi Yonoson Shteif (Figure 91). He was an acknowledged Talmudic scholar whose opinions on Jewish Law were solicited from far and wide. A very extensive text memorializing him is inscribed on this monument.

Our attention, however, is drawn to the inscription which is added:

> "Ho-even ha-zos asher samnu lee-ch'vod rabeinu matzay-voh
>   this monument which we have erected in honor of
>   our master
> ti-h'yeh gam l'zaycher bno u-ven v'no she-lo zochu lee-k'vuroh
>   shall also be as a memorial to his son and to his grandson
>   who were not granted burial
> v'ne-hergu al kiddush ha-Shem bee-y'may ha-milchomoh ha-no-ro-oh bee-sh'nos ha-domim
>   and were killed for the Sanctification of God's Name in
>   the time of the Great War in the era of bloody
>   destruction, 1944-1945
> Bno ho-rabonee, ha-muflag b'Torah u-v'yiras sho-maayim, morenu ho-rav Tzvi Yehuda, uvno ha-yeled Aharon Yitzchak, zichronom lee-v'rochoh. Ha-sho-chain bee-m'romim yizk'raym l'tovoh, v'yinkom domom
>   His son, the rabbinic scholar versed in Torah and
>   reverence, our master, Rabbi Tzvi Yehuda, and his son,
>   the lad Aharon Yitzchak, of blessed memory. May He
>   who dwells on High remember them for good, and may
>   their death be avenged."

Another extensive text is in memory of a righteous woman, Tushna Shpitzer, and on the bottom we behold a poignant inscription which describes her as a "righteous woman." It also includes a poignant memorial to her father:

> "L'zaycher olom nishmas ovinu hakodosh
>   In eternal memory of our saintly father
> morenu ho-rav Elazar Eliyahu ben moray-nu Ha-Rav Reuven ha-Cohen, ha-Shem yinkom domom
>   Our master the Rabbi Elazar, may his death be avenged
> she-nisfas bee-sh'nas tof-shin-daled al y'day ha-tzor-rim

who was caught by the persecutors in 1942
b'ays she-holach bee-m'siras nefesh la-a-seeyos tovos b'ad kehiloso
as he was engaged at great personal danger in a mission of good deeds on behalf of his community

v'lo noda k'vuroso
and his burial place is unknown
Yom ha Yahrzeit
the day of Yahrzeit is 8 Nisan 1945." (Figure 92)

So moving a story is couched in so cryptic a text...It is evident that the Rabbi was involved in a secret mission of great importance when he was caught by the oppressors and never seen again. Someone, however, lived to tell the tale, and inform his relatives of the date of his disappearance, which now is reverently observed as his *Yahrzeit*.

At the grave of Yehuda Frishman is a monument which has, on the bottom, an addition which is in some detail:

"*Ho-even ha-zos tee-h'yeh gam l'zaycher olom*
This monument shall also be an eternal remembrance
l'oviv ha-yokor morenu ho-rav
to our master Rabbi Meir son of Menache,
she-neherag al kiddush ha-Shem
who perished for the Sanctification of God's Name in Auschwitz, 10 Sivan 1944
v'lo zochoh l'kayver yisroel
and could not be given Jewish burial – may his death be avenged."

The last of this group is a monument for Tzvi Weiss, which also memorializes his father:

"*V'ho-even hazos ya-amod l'matzevas zikoron gam l'oviv*
And this monument will stand as a remembrance also for his father, Rabbi Meir ben Tzvi, may his death be avenged
mee-y'leeday Pressburg
native of Pressburg
she-olso nishmoso b'sa-arah ha-shmeemoh al kiddush ha-Shem

> *b'machanos ha-hash-modoh v'lo noda m'komo*
> whose soul arose in the raging destruction, for the Sanctification of God's Name, in the extermination camps, and his burial place is unknown."

Thus, the members of the ultra-orthodox Congregation Adas Y'rayim of Williamsburg, Brooklyn, evidence concern not only for those who lost their lives in the Holocaust, but also fulfilling for the rite of Jewish burial which was denied the martyrs.

We conclude this chapter with two memorials which, albeit not martyred, effectively memorialize their loved ones who were. These are posts holding the chain-link fence around an organizational plot. Each bears an inscription suitable for a monument. One is an extensive text indicating that the post is a gift of the brothers of the deceased It is specific in nature:

> "*She-nehergu, v'nish-ch'tu, v'nis-r'fu al kiddush ha-Shem may-ha-rotz-chim ha-Germanim ha-Nazim yimach sh-mom*
> who were killed, slaughtered and burned for the Sanctification of God's Name, by the German Nazis, may their names be erased
> *El Molay Rachamim-yinkom es nikmosom v'yimcheh es shmom v'es zichrom mee-tachas ha-shomayim*
> May the All-Merciful take vengeance upon the oppressors, and may their names and their remembrance be erased from beneath the Heavens."

Truly an inscription worthy of a major monument, rather than a modest and tiny fence post. The last example simply lists names of martyrs.

The nature, type and size of the memorials is varied and, seemingly, with no fixed pattern. The overriding motivation was to record a name, that it not be forgotten from the face of the earth. This volume is testimony to the fact that this goal was achieved.

CHAPTER ELEVEN
CONCLUSIONS AND RECOMMENDATIONS

This study has identified and described 148 monuments erected for martyrs of the Holocaust by organizations. They are located in sixteen cemeteries in the Greater New York metropolitan area. While the number of monuments may seem considerable, it would be wise to recognize that there are hundreds of landsmanshaften in the New York area that have not memorialized their kin by erecting a memorial on a cemetery.

It is my carefully considered opinion that I have found most of these organizational markers. As a practicing rabbi in New York, I have had occasion, alas too often, to officiate at funerals and unveilings at these cemeteries. I have been searching for these Holocaust memorials for many years. Somehow, I seem to have developed a detective's eye for them, and have trained myself to recognize them even from a distance. My observations and inquiries, I believe, have combined to give me a fairly accurate count. It is with little hesitation, therefore, that I assert that the number of memorials in respect to the number of organizations is relatively small.

It is importaant to note that the memorials which are standing do not draw attention to themselves. Only several in the entire study are set apart in such a way that a viewer will realize this monument is something special. Most of them are not constructed to deliberately attract attention. Even some of the most important monuments are so surrounded by many other family monuments that their effect is greatly diminished. It is obvious that little thought was given to placement, where they could best be seen by most people. Admittedly, practical consideration at most cemeteries, such as the cost of burial space, prevent or prohibit advantageous placement. By and large, therefore, their important message is unavoidably lost.

Several recommendations may be in order. First, the organizations should themselves erect some type of sign which states that a Holocaust Memorial is in place on their grounds (similar perhaps to the small signs placed at historical sites in Israel). Second, the cemetery management should be encouraged to erect a dignified and appropriate sign at a suitable place, perhaps in the office, stating that there are Holocaust memorials on this cemetery, and listing the locations of them. This would be considered a public service to the Jewish community and a suitable tribute to the martyrs.

Warsaw Ghetto & Resistance Organization, or American Federation of Jewish Fighters, Camp Inmates & Nazi Victims might be the organizations who could be approached to contact cemeteries in this regard.

Another observation. The purpose of a memorial is to insure remembrance. As we walk through the cemeteries and view these monuments we note that most of the meaningful and descriptive inscriptions are in Yiddish or Hebrew. Many have no English at all, some only several lines, often not a true translation. This means that the effect of these memorials will not make an impression to American Jews who are not conversant with either language.

The overwhelming majority of those who see these monuments will know only English. The members of the landsmanshaften are aware of this. They know that few of their own children understand Yiddish, and almost none read it. They know that the same is true, more so, of their children's knowledge of Hebrew. And what of their grandchildren? It is a painful statement to make, but sadly true.

It is my feeling, therefore, based on this study, that there should be an English translation of Yiddish or Hebrew text adjacent to each monument, *"l'ma-an yaydu"* so that the modern generation "should know" what befell our people, and how that catastrophe was memorialized here in our area.

Finally, one element in this study deserves special mention. This is the practice described in Chapter 10. A person dies, is buried and a monument is erected over the grave. On that monument is added a special inscription for family members who perished in the Holocaust. Note the examples in Figures 86 to 92. Here, too, some are extensive and explicit, and some are very general, mentioning only names.

In my opinion that is a practice to be recommended. There are many families among us who have lost loved ones in the Holocaust for whom there is no memorial. This is a most suitable manner to memorialize them.

As it turned out, I found these added memorials almost exclusively on the grounds of religious groups, such as synagogues and chevras. A great number were from the chassidic community, as indicated by the markers for rebbes on those grounds. It seems evident that most such organizations members immigrated to the United States either just before, during, or just after World War II and, therefore, had immediate family members who did not survive. Such people were probably closer in body and spirit to the tragedy and may have felt more compelled to add the memorial inscription. Whether this is so or not, it is certain that the incidence of such inscriptions is overwhelmingly larger among the orthodox groups than others.

May the remembrance of the Holocaust help insure that a repetition will never occur.

APPENDIX

APPENDIX 1

Alphabetical list of organizations and the cemeteries where their Holocaust memorials are located.
Page numbers in parenthesis.

ANTIPOLIA (36)
Old Montefiore Cemetery
Springfield Gardens, New York

BARYSZER (74)
New Montefiore Cemetery
Pinelawn, Long Island

BENDIN-SOSNOWICER (28)
Beth Israel Cemetery
Woodbridge, New Jersey

BUKACZOWZER (78)
Mt. Hebron Cemetery
Flushing, New York

BURSTYNER (68)
Wellwood Cemetery
Pinelawn, Long Island

CHMIELNIK (59)
Beth Israel Cemetery
Woodbridge, New York

CHODOROWER (52)
Mt. Hebron Cemetery
Flushing, New York

CRACOWER (47)
Beth Moses Cemetery
Pinelawn, Long Island

DINEWITZER (36)
New Montefiore Cemetery
Pinelawn, Long Island

DISNER (57)
Old Montefiore Cemetery
Springfield Gardens, New York

DOMBROVER (52)
United Hebrew Cemetery
Staten Island, New York

DROBNINER (25)
Mt. Hebron Cemetery
Flushing, New York

DROHOBYCZER and BORYSLAWER (40)
New Montefiore Cemetery
Pinelawn, Long Island

EAST SIDE SOCIAL CENTER (23)
King Solomon Cemetery
Clifton, New Jersey

EISHISHOK (174)
United Hebrew Cemetery
Staten Island, New York

GLOBOKER (55)
New Montefiore Cemetery
Pinelawn, Long Island

GRODNER (34)
Mt. Hebron Cemetery
Flushing, New York

GRODZISKER (61)
United Hebrew Cemetery
Staten Island, New York

GRYBOWER (39)
King Solomon Cemetery
Clifton, New Jersey

HRUBIESHOW (69,71)
New Montefiore Cemetery
Pinelawn, Long Island

ISBITZE (73)
Old Montefiore Cemetery
Springfield Gardens, New York

JAWOROWER (57)
Beth Moses Cemetery
Pinelawn, New York

KIELTZER (38)
New Montefiore Cemetery
Pinelawn, Long Island

KOBRINER (42)
Mt. Judah Cemetery
Ridgewood, New York

KOLBUSZOWA (30)
Beth Israel Cemetery
Woodbridge, New Jersey

KOSSOVER (56)
New Montefiore Cemetery
Pinelawn, Long Island

KUZMINER-VOLINER (38)
New Montefiore Cemetery
Pinelawn, Long Island

LANZUT (58)
Mt. Judah Cemetery
Ridgewood, New York

LEBEDOWE and RADZILOWE (76)
Wellwood Cemetery
Pinelawn, Long Island

LECHOWITZ (40)
Beth David Cemetery
Elmont, Long Island

LITINER (46)
Mt. Hebron Cemetery
Flushing, New York

LODZER (45)
New Montefiore Cemetery
Pinelawn, Long Island

LOKATCHER (74)
Beth David Cemetery
Elmont, Long Island

MALATER (68)
Beth David Cemetery
Elmont, Long Island

MARIAMPOL (65)
Old Montefiore Cemetery
Springfield Gardens, New York

MOLODETSNER (76)
Wellwood Cemetery
Pinelawn, Long Island

NARAJOW (55)
Beth David Cemetery
Eimont, Long Island

NAREVKE (72)
Mt. Hebron Cemetery
Flushing, New York

NEMIROWER (39)
Beth David Cemetery
Elmont, Long Island

NOVA USHITZA (54)
Beth David Cemetery
Elmont, Long Island

OSTROVER (54)
Beth David Cemetery
Elmont, Long Island

OTYNIER (33)
New Montefiore Cemetery
Pinelawn, Long Island

PILTZER (55)
Wellwood Cemetery
Pinelawn, Long Island

PLANCHER (57)
New Montefiore Cemetery
Pinelawn, Long Island

POLONER (57)
Baron de Hirsch Cemetery
Staten Island, New York

POMORZANER (76)
Beth Moses Cemetery
Pinelawn, Long Island

RADOMER (27)
New Montefiore Cemetery
Pinelawn, Long Island

RHODES LEAGUE OF BROTHERS (59)
Beth Israel Cemetery
Woodbridge, New Jersey

ROTCHEV (35)
Old Montefiore Cemetery
Springfield Gardens, New York

ROVNER (35)
Beth David Cemetery
Elmont, Long Island

RYPINER (39)
Baron de Hirsch Cemetery
Staten Island, New York

SAMBORER (34)
Old Montefiore Cemetery
Springfield Gardens, New York

SASSOWER (33,41,42)
Wellwood Cemetery
Pinelawn, Long Island

SHEBRESHIN (69)
New Montefiore Cemetery
Pinelawn, Long Island

SERHEIER (59)
Mt. Judah Cemetery
Ridgewood, New York

SKARZYSKO (57)
Baron de Hirsch Cemetery
Staten Island, New York

SKIDEL (71)
Beth Israel Cemetery
Woodbridge, New Jersey

SINOVER (63)
Mt. Hebron Cemetery
Flushing, New York

SOLOTWINER (61)
Mt. Hebron Cemetery
Flushing, New York

TITCHINER (73)
Beth David Cemetery
Elmont, Long Island

TRISK-VOLIN (65)
Beth David Cemetery
Elmont, Long Island

VINITZE (84)
Old Montefiore
Springfield Gardens, New York

WISHNEWITZ-VOLIN (79)
Mt. Hebron Cemetery
Flushing, New York

WLADOWER (77)
New Montefiore Cemetery
Pinelawn, Long Island

WLODZIMIEREZ (35)
Beth David Cemetery
Elmont, New York

WOLOCHISK (34)
Old Montefiore Cemetery
Springfield Gardens, New York

YIDDISH MAYDEN (57)
Beth David Cemetery
Elmont, Long Island

YOSEFOV (33,41,42)
New Montefiore Cemetery
Pinelawn, Long Island

ZBARAZ (42)
Beth David Cemetery
Elmont, Long Island

ZDUNSKA-WOLA (57)
Baron de Hirsch Cemetery
Staten Island, New York

ZEZMER (74)
Beth David Cemetery
Elmont, Long Island

ZINKOV (53,54)
Old Montefiore Cemetery
Springfield Gardens, New York

ZLOCZOWER (74)
New Montefiore Cemetery
Pinelawn, Long Island

APPENDIX 1A
List of photographs that were not available when text was completed. See Appendix 9
Pages are in parenthesis.

APTER (158)
AUSTILER (145)
BARANOW (146)
BARANOWICH (146)
BELCHETOW (146)
BIALOBRZEGI (148)
B'NAI ISRAEL (172)
BOCHINA-WISHNITZ
    BRIGEL (147)
BODKER (147)
BRITCHAN (147)
BROHILOVER (148)
BUDZANOWER (162)
(NEW) CRACOW (149, 150)
CHYROW (148)
DOMBIER (151)
DUCOR (163)
EISHISOK (174)
FALENCIA (151)
GERMAN PERSECUTION
    SURVIVORS (152)
GONIONDZ and TRESTINE (151)
GRAMBOWER, KLODOWER (152)
GRYBOWER (157)
HUSIATYNER (163)
JAGIELNICER (152)
JEWISH WAR VETERANS (158)
KALUSHIN (153)
KIELTZER CHILDREN (159)
KONSTANTIN (154)
KORELITZER (155)
KRASHNIK (153)
KRYSTYNOPOLER (172)
KUNIVER (154)

LASK (155)
LIBOVNER VOLINER (154)
LODZER (162)
LUBER (156)
LUKOWER (157)
MAGIEV (156)
MELNICE (165)
MEDGIBOSH (161)
MIECHOVER (161)
MOSCISKER (156)
OSTROWCER (161)
OZORKOWER (165)
PAVIANCER (160)
PECHOWITZ (164)
PLONSK (160)
PODHAJCE (160)
PRZEMYSL (159)
RADOMER (163, 164, 166)
ROZDOL (173)
SCHACTER FAMILY (175)
SHERSHOW (173)
SKERNIEWICE (167)
SKOLER (162)
SOKOLOV-PODLASKI (167)
SOKOLOVER-
   LEJENSKER (167)
SOROKER (170)
TARNOV (157)
TCHUDNOW (168)
TOMASZOW (169)
TRZEBINA (169)
TYSZOWITZER (169)
WLADOWER (170)
YUGOSLAV JEWS (171)
ZAMOSC (158, 172)

APPENDIX 2
LIST OF CEMETERIES AND LOCATION OF ORGANIZATION PLOTS

BARON HIRSCH CEMETERY
Staten Island, New York

POLONER	SEC B
RYPINER	SEC G
SKARZYSKO	SEC J
ZDUNSKA-WOLA	SEC B
SCHNEIDERMAN-WAKSMAN FAMILIES	SEC ???

BETH DAVID CEMETERY
ELMONT, LONG ISLAND

LECHOWITZ	BL C5
LOKATCHER	BL A8
LUDMIR	BL A3
MALATER	BL AA4
NARAJOW	BL G4
NEMIROWER	BL A8
NOVA USHITZA	SEC 1-4
OSTROVER	BL A6
ROVNER	BL E4
STOLINER	BL A2
TARNOPOL	BL F3
TITCHINER	BL AA7
TRISK-VOLIN	BL A10
YIDDISH MAYDEN	SEC 1-4
ZBARAZ	BL AA1
ZEZMER	BL B2
BALABAN FAMILY	BL E5
FARKASH FAMILY	BL G2
HIRSCHBAUM FAMILY	BL AB

BETH ISRAEL CEMETERY
WOODBRIDGE, New Jersey

BENDIN-SOSNOWICER	BL 50
CHMIELNIK	BL 5
KOLBUSZOWA	BL 6
RHODES LEAGUE OF BROTHERS	BL 51
SKIDEL	BL 2

BETH MOSES
PINELAWN, LONG ISLAND

CRACOWER	EL 10
JAWOROWER	EL 18
POMORZANER	BL 14
OTYNIER	BL 29

KING SOLOMON CEMETERY
CLIFTON, NEW JERSEY

EAST SIDE SOCIAL CTR	GILBOA BL
GRYBOWER	JUDEA EL

OLD MONTEFIORE CEMETERY
SPRINGFIELD GARDENS, NEW YORK

ANTIPOLIA	BL 85
DISNER	EL 86
ISBITZE	EL 93
LIPNER	EL 80
MARIAMPOL	EL 86
ROTCHEV	BL 9
SAMBORER	EL 79
WOLOCHISK	EL 81
ZINKOV	EL 94
AKAPNIK FAMILY	EL 81
DEREN FAMILY	EL 85
PESACH NOTTE FAMILY	EL 97

MT. HEBRON CEMETERY
FLUSHING, New York

BUKACZOWZER	BL 80
CHODOROWER	BL 52
DOMBROWER	BL 10
GRODNER	BL 19
LITINER PODOLIER	BL 24
NAREVKE	BL 5
SINOVER	BL 54
SOLOTWINER	BL 65
WISHNEWITZ-VOLIN	BL 76 D

NEW MT. CARMEL CEMETERY
RIDGEWOOD, NEW YORK

ZYGELBOIM	SEC B-10 C
NOWOGRODSKI FAMILY	SEC B-10 E
WASSER FAMILY	SEC B-10 E

MT. JUDAH CEMETERY
RIDGEWOOD, NEW YORK

KOBRINER	BL 1
LANZUT	BL 4
SERHEIER	BL 4

NEW MONTEFIORE CEMETERY
PINELAWN, LONG ISLAND

DINEWITZER-PODOLIER	SEC 6 BL 9
DROHOBYCZER and BORYSLAWER	SEC 5 BL 13
GLOBOKER	SEC 3 BL 14
HRUBIESHOW	SEC 3 BL 5
KIELTZER	SEC 6 BL 10
KOSSOVER	SEC 6 BL 1
KUZMINER-VOLINER	SEC 5 BL 6
LEDOWE and RADZILOWE	SEC 4 BL 10

LODZER	SEC 4 BL 16
MOLODETSNER	SEC 6 BL 13
PLANCHER	SEC 6 BL 11
RADOMER	SEC 4 BL 3
SHEBRESHIN	SEC 3 BL 15
WLADOWER	SEC 3 BL 3
YOSEFOV	SEC 4 BL 16
ALTMAN FAMILY	SEC 5 BL 12
BARISH FAMILY	SEC 3 BL 12
BREGSTEIN FAMILY	
KOTNER FAMILY	
LIFSHITZ FAMILY	
SHLOMTZI FAMILY	SEC 5 BL 12
WIENER FAMILY	

WELLWOOD CEMETERY
PINELAWN, LONG ISLAND

BARYSZER	BL 44
BURSTYNER	BL 13
MOLODETSNER	BL 47
PILTZER	BL 47
SASSOWER	BL 42
ZLOCZOWER	BL 47

UNITED HEBREW CEMETERY
STATEN ISLAND, NEW YORK

DROENINER	BL 104
GRODZISKER	BL 127
EISHISHOK	BL 36

APPENDIX 3
MAPS OF CEMETERIES
WITH LOCATIONS OF MONUMENTS
(Locations are marked by
Star of David [✡] or Bullet [•]

Baron Hirsch Cemetery
Staten Island, NY

BLOCK
C14	Poloner	Sec. B
B12	Rypiner	Sec. G
C15	Skarzysko	Sec. J
C13	Zdunska-Wola	Sec, B
F3	Schneiderman-Waksman Families	Sec. C

Beth El - Cedar Park
Paramus, NJ

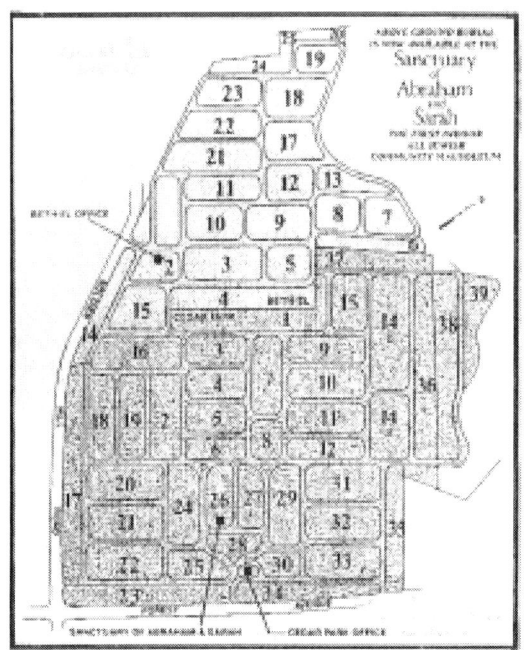

Beth El
Berliner
Tomaszow-Maz
Trestine
Goniondzer-Trestiner
Washington Heights Cong.
Zamosc

Cedar Park
Ducor
Kopshitz - BL9

Beth David Cemetery
Elmont, Long Island, NY

BLOCK	ORGANIZATION
C5	Lechowitz
A8	Lokatcher
A3	Ludmir
AA4	Malater
G4	Narajow
A8	Nemirower
SecOne-4	Nova Ushitza
A6	Ostrover
E4	Rovner
A2	Stoliner
F3	Tarnopol
AA7	Titchiner
A10	Tristk-Volin
SecOne-4	Yiddish Mayden
AA1	Zbaraz
B2	Zezmer
A5	Balaban Family
G2	Farkash Family
A8	Hirschbaum Family
B7	Bodker
B8	Budzanower
	Devenishok
B10	Lask
G6	Marmarosh
	Medgibosh
	Ostropolier
	Plonsk
	Przemysl
	Tchudnow
	Bochina/Wishnitz/Brigel

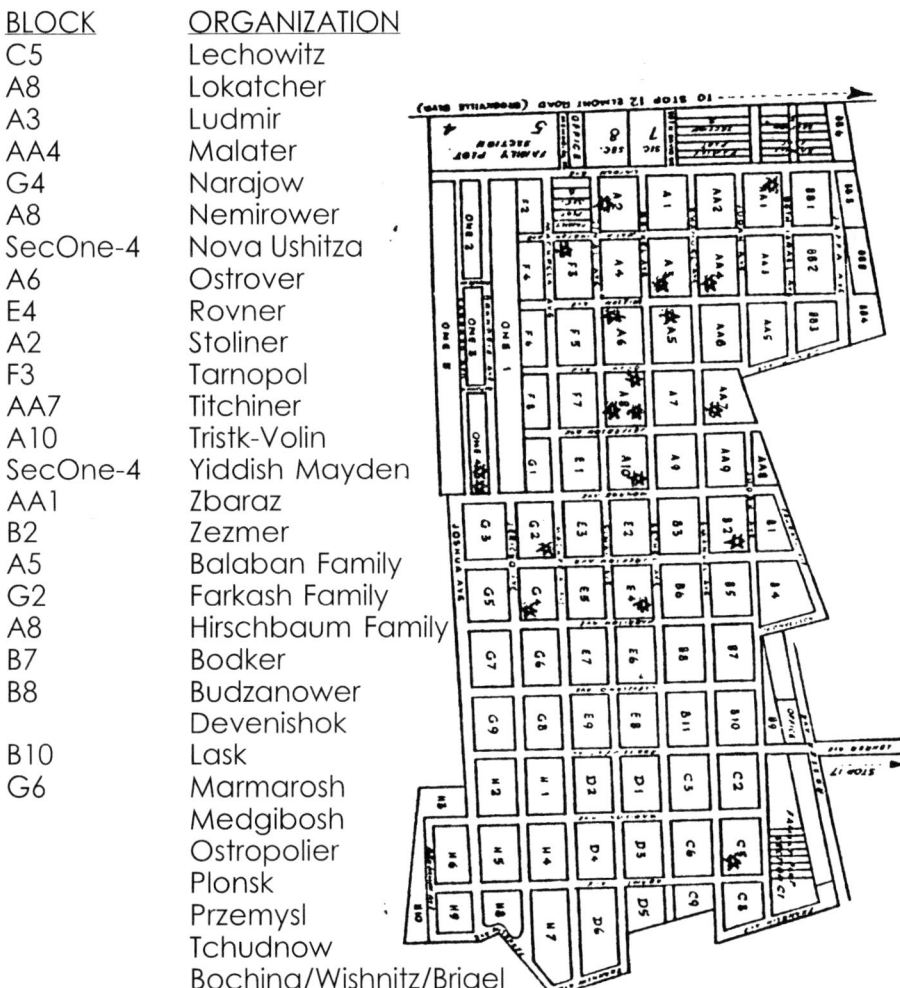

Beth Israel Cemetery
Woodbridge, NJ

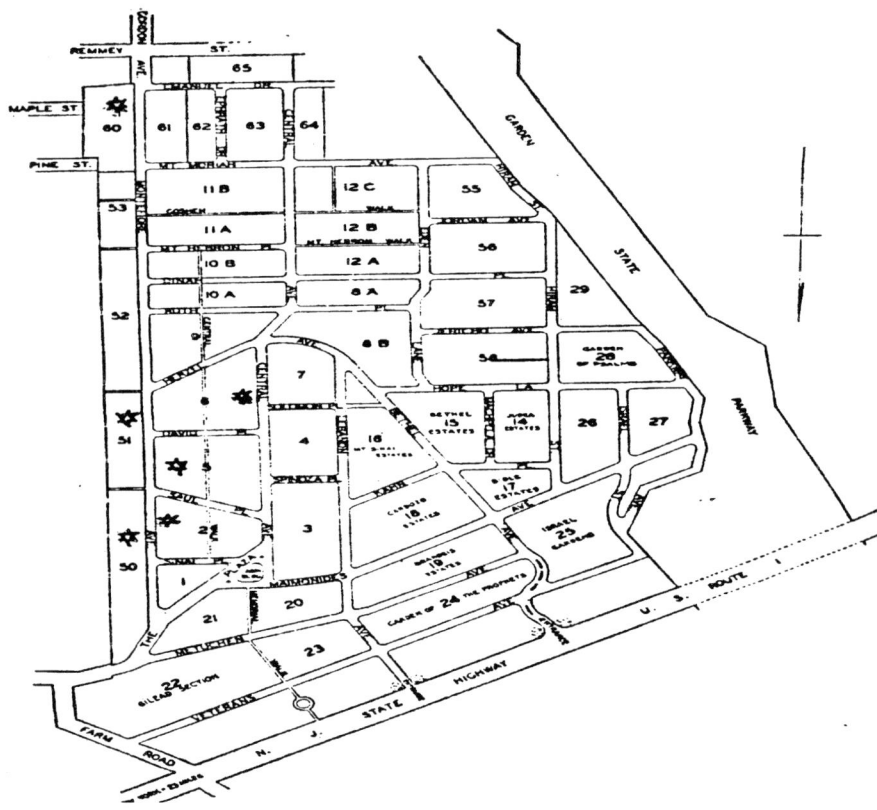

BLOCK	ORGANIZATION
50	Bendin-Sosnowicer
5	Chmielnik
6	Kolboszowa
51	Rhodes League of Brothers
2	Skidel
60	Rabbi Steiff
64	Plotrikin

Beth Moses Cemetery
Farmingdale, NY

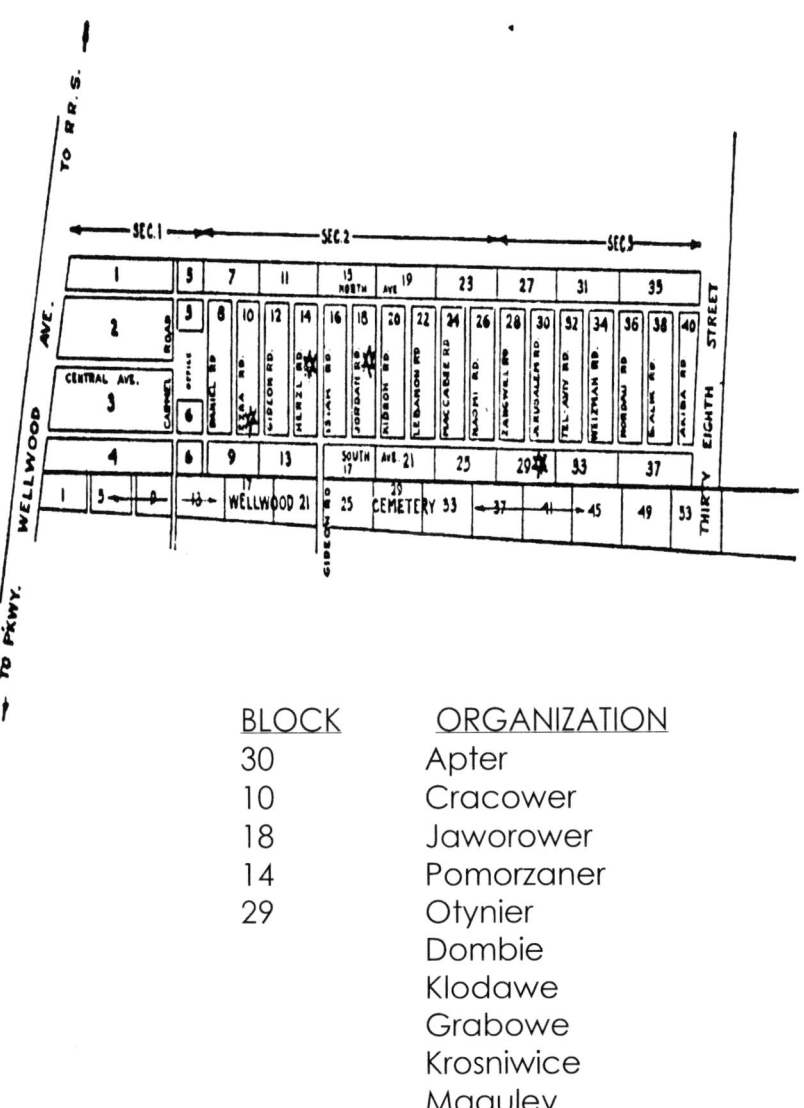

BLOCK	ORGANIZATION
30	Apter
10	Cracower
18	Jaworower
14	Pomorzaner
29	Otynier
	Dombie
	Klodawe
	Grabowe
	Krosniwice
	Magulev

King Solomon Cemetery
Clifton, NJ

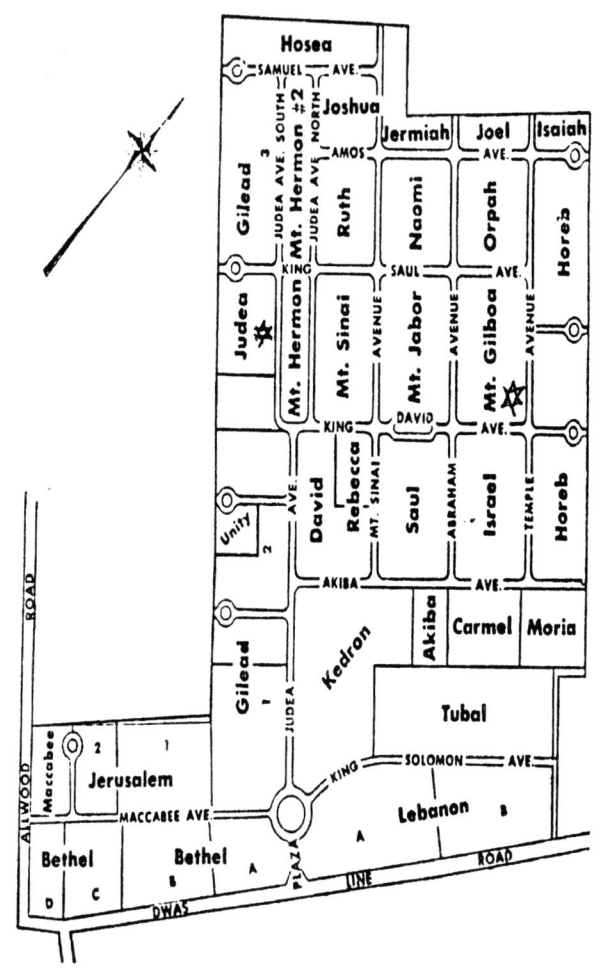

Gilboa Block

Judea Block

East Side Social Center of Paterson, NJ

Grybower

Montefiore (Old) Cemetery
Laurelton, NY

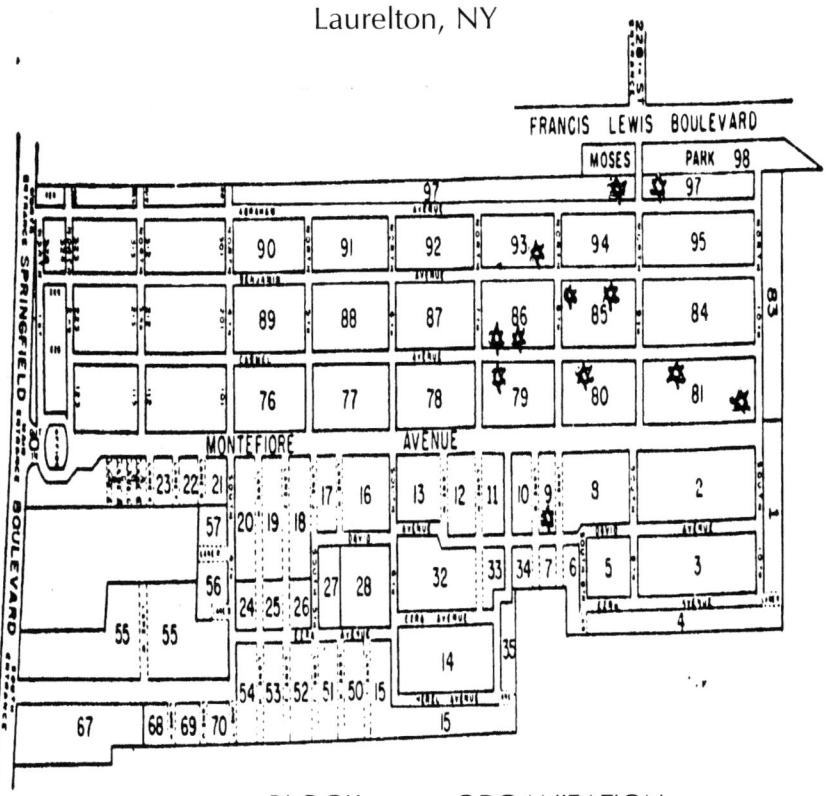

BLOCK	ORGANIZATION
85	Anti Polia
86	Disner
93	Isbitze
80	Lipner
86	Mariapol
9	Rotchev
79	Samborer
81	Wolochisk
94	Zinkov
81	Akapnik Family
85	Deren Family
97	Pesach Notte Family
15	Sernicker
67	Strelisker Britchan

Mt. Hebron Cemetery
Flushing, NY

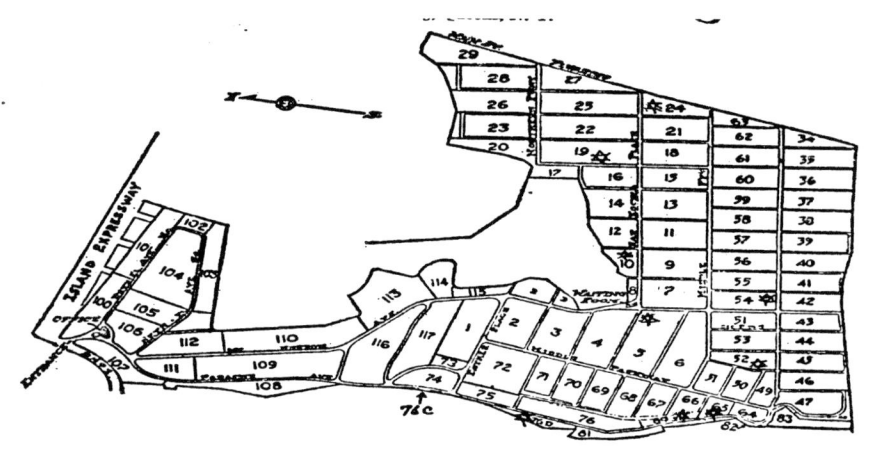

BLOCK	ORGANIZATION
80	Bukaczowzer
52	Chodorower
10	Dombrower
19	Grodner
24	Litiner-Podolier
5	Narevke
54	Sinover
65	Solotwiner
76D	Wishnewitz-Volin
	Belchetow
	Jagielnicer
	Rozdol

Mount Judah Cemetery
Ridgewood, NY

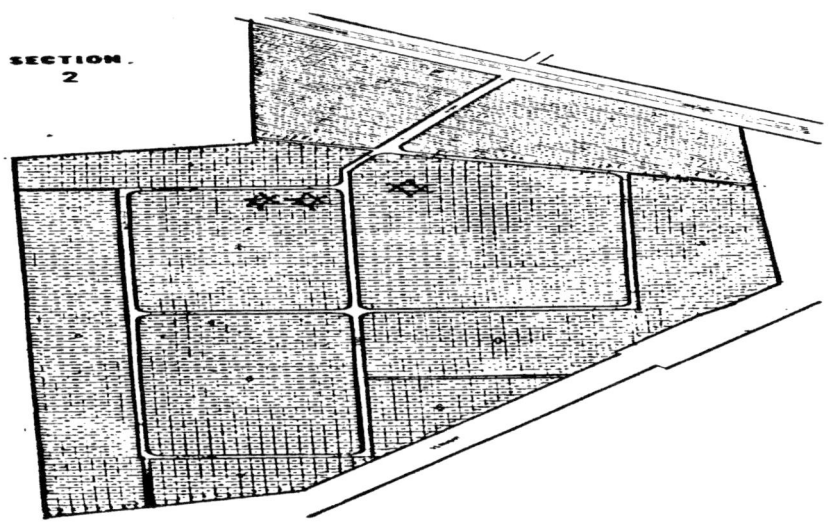

BLOCK	ORGANIZATION
1	Kobriner
BL4	Lanzut
BL4	Serheier

New Mt. Carmel Cemetery
Ridgewood, NY

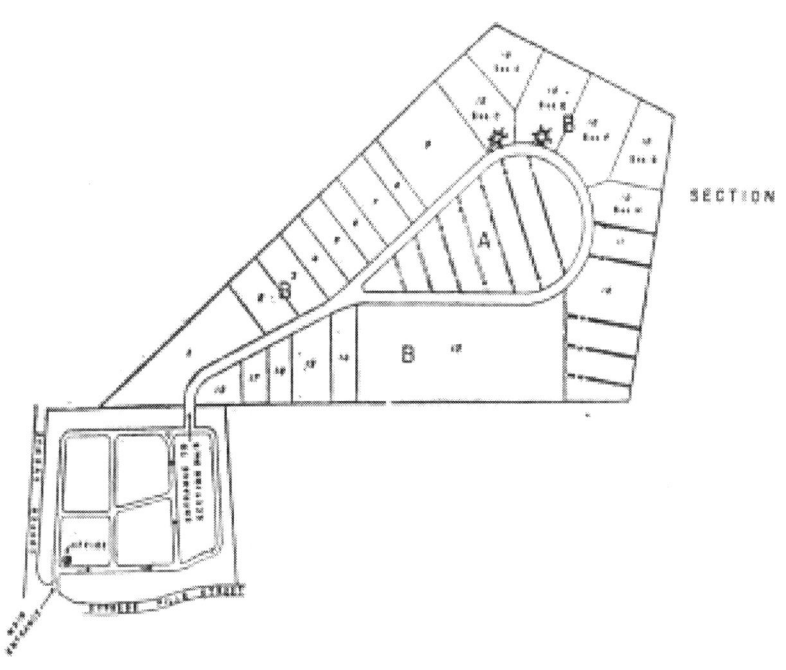

SECTION 3 AREA B
BL10C   Zygelboim
BL10E   Nowogrodski Family
          Wasser Family

New Montefiore Cemetery
Wellwood, NY

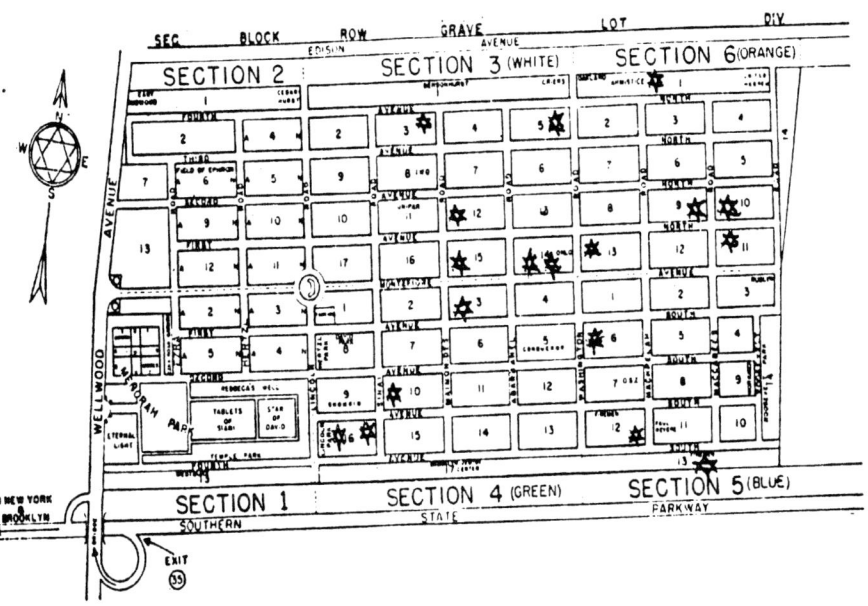

Sec. 6	BL 9	Dinewitzer-Podolier	Sec. 6	BL 7	Baranower
Sec. 5	BL 13	Drohbyczer &			Kieltz
		Boryslawer			Krashnik
Sec. 3	BL 14	Globoker			Korelitzer
Sec. 3	BL 5	Hrubieshow			Lubar
Sec. 5	BL 10	Kieltzer			Miechover
Sec. 6	BL 1	Kossover			Moscisker
Sec. 5	BL 6	Kuzminer-Voliner			Nevstadter
Sec. 5	BL 12	Altman Family			Ostrowiecz
Sec. 3	BL 12	Barish Family			New Konstantin
Sec. 3	BL 14	Bregstein Family			Puchowitz
Sec. 3	BL 14	Kotner Family	Sec. 5	BL 4	Rawa Ruska
Sec. 3	BL 14	Lifshitz Family			Shershower
Sec. 5	BL 12	Shlomtzi Family	Sec. 4	BL 14	Sokolifker
Sec. 3	BL 14	Wiener Family			Sokolov-Podalski

Mt. Moriah
Fairview, NJ

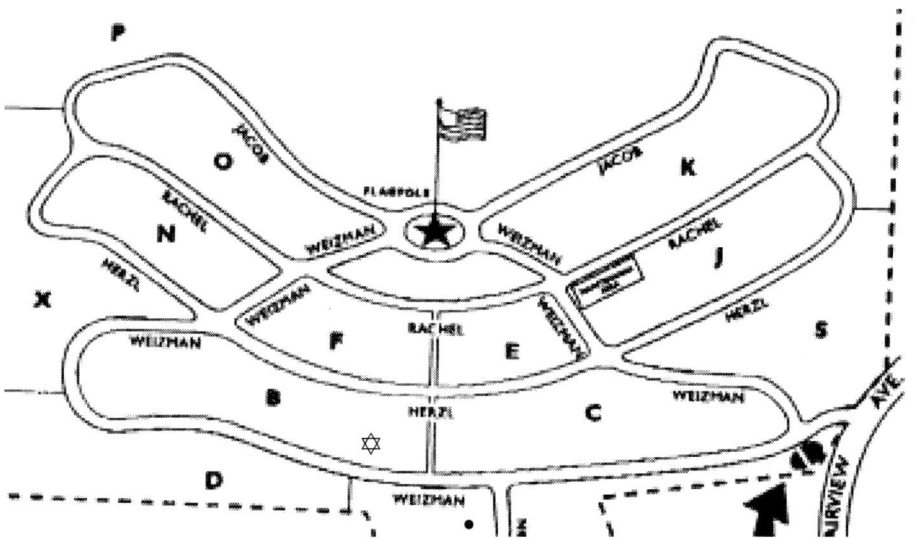

Sec. A	BL 15	Austiler
Div. B		Brohilover
		Falencia
Sec. B	BL 10	Pabiance
		Skerniewice
Sec. X	BL 6	Association/
		Yugoslav Jews

Wellwood Cemetery
Pinelawn, NY

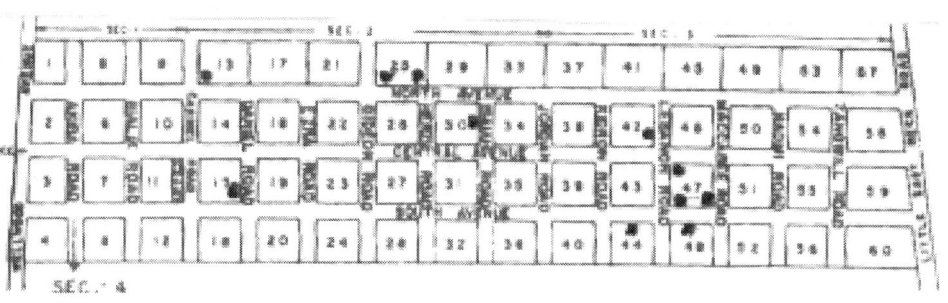

BLOCK	ORGANIZATION
44	Baryszer
13	Burstyner
47	Molodetsner
47	Piltzer
42	Sassower
47	Zloczower
48	Baranowicher
25	Chotiner
30	Chyrower & Felszstyn
1	Janina (Section 4)
25	Zalanow

United Hebrew Cemetery
Richmond, Staten Island

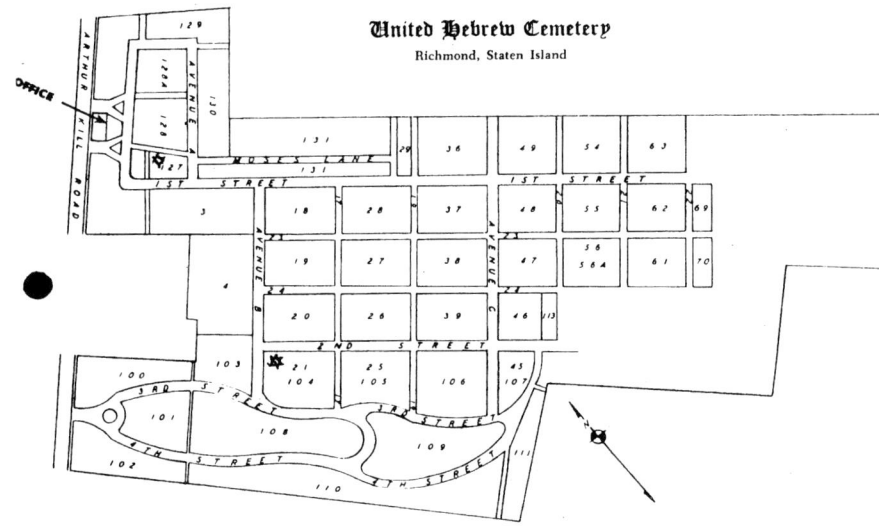

BLOCK	ORGANIZATION
104	Drobniner
127	Grodzisker
36	Eishishok
	Kalushin
	Libovner
	Lukower
	Tyszowitzer

APPENDIX 4
DATES WHEN ORGANIZATION MONUMENTS WERE ERECTED

ORGANIZATION	DATE
LITINER	1947
ZBARAZ	1947
GRYBOWER	1947
RYPINER	1947
KOLBUSZOWA	1948
ANTIPOLIA	1948
SOLOTWINER	1949
NAREVKE	1951
ROVNER	1954
ZDUNSKA WOLA	1954
KIELTZER	1957
OSTROVER	1959
RADOMER	1960
DROBNINER	1961
LECHOWITZ	1961
DISNER	1964
NEMIROWER	1966
HRUBIESHOW	1966
POMORZANER	1967
PLANCHER	1967
EAST SIDE SOCIAL CTR	1967
CRACOWER	1969
LODZER	1976
GLOBOKER	1980

APPENDIX 5
ORGANIZATION MONUMENTS THAT SPECIFY NUMBER OF MARTYRS

ORGANIZATION	NO. KILLED
ANTIPOLIA	2,500
CHODOROWER	1,700
GRODZISKER	5,000
GRYBOWER	360
KIELTZER	28,000
KOLBUSZOWA	1,800
LECHOWITZ	4,000
LITINER	3,940
LUDMIR	20,000
NEMIROWER	6,000
RADOMER	30,000
ROVNER	23,500
SAMBORER	8,000
ZBARAZER	3,142

APPENDIX 6
ORGANIZATIONS WHICH SPECIFY DATE OF YAHRZEIT

ORGANIZATION	YAHRZEIT
BUKACZOWZER	YOM KIPPUR
DISNER	2 TAMMUZ
DROBNINER 1	4 KISLEV
KIELTZER	9 ELUL
KUZMINER-VOLINER	TISHA B'AV
LANZUT	21 AV
LOKATCHER	27 ELUL
MARIAMPOL	YOM KIPPUR
PLANCHER	6 CHESHVAN
SERHEIER	28 ELUL
TRISK-VOLIN	12 ELUL
WISHNEWITZ-ZVOLYN	EVE OF ROSH HASHONAH
YIDDISH MAYDEN	YOM KIPPUR

APPENDIX 7
MONUMENTS WHICH SPECIFICALLY MENTION NAZIS BY NAME

BARYSZER
BENDIN-SOSNOWICZER
CHMIELNIK
CRACOWER
DINEWITZER PODOLIER
DROBNINER
DROHOBYCZER & BORYSLAWER
EAST SIDE SOCIAL CENTER
GRYBOWER
HRUBIESHOW *(Mentions Hitler)*
KIELTZER
LECHOWITZ
LOKATCHER
MALATER
MOLODETSNER
NAREVKE
NOVA USHITZA
PLANCHER
POLONER
POMORZANER
RADOMER
SKIDEL
SINOVER
TITCHINER
TRISK-VOLIN
WISHNEWITZ-VOLYN
WLADOWER
WOLOCHISK
YIDDISH MAYDEN
ZBARAZ
ZEZMER
ZLOCZOWER

AKAPNIK
ALTMAN
PESACH NOTTE

APPENDIX 8

AN INTRODUCTION TO AN ELEGY

Included here, most appropriately, is an elegy for the Six Million, composed by Rabbi Simon Schwab, z"l, in 1954. It is printed in the Tisha B'Av prayer book of Mesorah Publications, Inc., with an English translation by Rabbi Avrohom Chaim Feuer and Rabbi Avie Gold.

The elegy is appropriate to this volume, because it is in itself a major memorial. It is as important as the monuments herein described, if not more so. The monuments are silent testimony to the Great Tragedy, while the elegy speaks aloud. It is recited annually on what our Sephardic brethren call the Black Fast, Tisha B'Av, the most sorrowful day in the Jewish calendar.

It should be noted for the record that Rav Schwab never saw this book and voiced no opinion as to the propriety of the language of the texts on the monuments and plaques shown herein.

The text in Hebrew and English is excerpted from *The Complete Tishah B'Av Service* by Rabbi Avrohom Chaim Feuer and Rabbi Avie Gold. © by Artscroll / Mesorah Publications Ltd. Reprinted with permission.

הַזּוֹכֵר *He, Who remembers.* Rav Shimon Schwab, שליט״א, widely recognized as an eloquent spokesman for Torah Jewry, joined the Rabbinate of Congregation Khal Adas Jeshurun in the Washington Heights neighborhood of New York, in 1958, in association with the late revered Rav Dr. Joseph Breuer, זצ״ל.

Rav Schwab was born in Frankfurt-am-Main, Germany in 1908, and studied at several well-known Eastern European *yeshivos,* including Telshe and Mir. In those years, Rav Schwab had the opportunity to meet with and learn from the foremost *Gedolim* of the time, including the holy Chafetz Chaim of Radin.

In the early 1930s Rav Schwab was an eyewitness to the rise of Hitler Nazism in Germany and the systematic oppression of the Jews. In 1936, the persecution of the Nazis forced him to leave his pulpit in Germany. He came to the United States where he assumed a position in the Baltimore Rabbinate.

Rav Schwab relates that in 1959, as Tishah B'Av approached, the late Rav Breuer made a request of him, "Please compose a special Tishah B' Av *kinnah* for our *kehillah.* Each and everyone of us is either a refugee or a Holocaust survivor. We have all lost family and friends in this *churban,* and we German Jews bore the brunt of Hitler's fury. We must not forget, nor can we allow our children to forget. Eight centuries ago German Jewry was slaughtered by the Crusaders.

"According to historians, how many Jews were killed? Perhaps 5,000. In World War II more than one thousand times that number were killed! In just one day at Aushchwitz more than 5,000 Jews were brutally gassed and murdered. If German Jewry composed kinos to commemorate the evil that befell us during the Crusades, how much more so must we compose one over the Holocaust!"

In deference to this request, Rav Schwab composed the following *kinnah* which, in Khal Adas Jeshurun, is recited by the Rav on Tishah B'Av night at the conclusion of the *kinnos* service after the passage which begins with תרחם ציון *Have mercy on Zion.* Although Rav Schwab only composed this *kinnah* to be said in his *kehillah,* many other congregations have adopted the custom of reciting it on Tishah B'Av, either at night or by day, as a memorial of our most recent *Churban.*

הַזּוֹכֵר מַזְכִּירָיו,   דּוֹר דּוֹר וְקָדוֹשָׁיו,
מֵעֵת אֲשֶׁר אָז בְּחַרְתָּנוּ,
יִזְכּוֹר בְּרָאוֹן,   שֶׁל דּוֹר אַחֲרוֹן,
אוֹיָה מֶה הָיָה לָּנוּ.

שְׁטוּפֵי מַבּוּל דָּם,   שֶׁמָּסְרוּ נַפְשׁוֹתָם,
כָּל שְׁקוּעֵי עִמְקֵי הַבָּכָא,
יִפְקְדֵם אֱלֹהִים,   בְּאַרְצוֹת הַחַיִּים,
וְעָרֵי עַד זָכְרֵם לִבְרָכָה.

שְׂאוּ אֵלָיו כַּפַּיִם,   אֲהָהּ, אִי שָׁמַיִם,
הוֹי עַל מֵיטַב שִׁבְטֵי יִשְׂרָאֵל,
עֵדוֹת וּקְהִלּוֹת,   עָרִים וּגְלִילוֹת,
חֲבוּרוֹת, מוֹסָדוֹת, כָּל מוֹעֲדֵי אֵל.

מִי יִתֵּן פַּלְגֵי מַיִם,   תֵּרַדְנָה עֵינַיִם,
אֶל אֲשֵׁדוֹת נַחֲלֵי הַדְּמָעוֹת,
עֲלֵי אַלְפֵי אֲלָפִים,   גּוּפִים נִשְׂרָפִים,
בְּמוֹ אֵשׁ הַחֻרְבָּן וּזְנָעוֹת.

הזוכר He, Who remembers those who remember Him,
   Each generation and its holy ones —
since the time You have chosen us —
May He remember the gruesome fate
of the last generation.
Woe! what has happened to us!

Those who were swept away by the flood of blood —
who sacrificed their lives —
All who were submerged in valleys of tears,
May God think of them in the lands of eternal life.
May their memory be a blessing for all eternity.

Lift up your hands to Him, woe O you Heavens!
Woe over the best of Israel's tribes,
Communities and congregations, cities and districts,
fraternities, foundations, all rendezvous with God.

If only streams of water could pour down from eyes
towards waterfalls of the rivers of tears,
for the thousands times thousands of corpses
consumed in the fire of destructions and horrors.

וְעַל שָׂרֵי הַתּוֹרָה,   וּמַחֲזִיקֵי מָסוֹרָה,
וְעַל פִּרְחֵי הַכְּהֻנָּה הַצְּעִירִים,
וְעַל חוֹבְשֵׁי מִדְרָשׁוֹת,   וּמוֹרִים וּמוֹרוֹת,
תִּינוֹקוֹת בֵּית רַבָּן יְקִירִים.
עַל בָּנוֹת בּוֹטְחוֹת,   וְסָבִים וְסָבוֹת,
וְעַל זַרְעָם וְטַפָּם שֶׁיָּלְדוּ,
וְגַם לִרְבָבוֹת,   רִבְבוֹת נֶאֱהָבִים בַּחַיִּים,
בְּמוֹתָם לֹא נִפְרָדוּ.
אֶת דָּמָם דְּרוֹשׁ,   כִּי תִשָּׂא אֶת רֹאשׁ,
שֶׁל כָּל נִדָּף לֶעָלִים הַטְּרוּפִים.
כָּל נַפְשׁוֹת מֵת,   בִּימֵי שֶׁבֶר וָשֹׁאת,
שִׁשָּׁה אַלְפֵי פְּעָמִים אֲלָפִים.
שְׁלִישִׁיָּה לְבָעֵר,   בְּבָרָק וְעִם סוֹעֵר,
מִכַּרְמֵי הַחֶמֶד אֲהַבְתָּ.
גּוֹאֵל הַדָּם,   נָא זְכֹר צַעֲרָם,
אַל תִּמְחֶה מִסְפַּר כָּתַבְתָּ.
זְכֹר הַנְאָקוֹת,   וְרַעַשׁ צְעָקוֹת,
אָז יוּבְלוּ לָרֶצַח,
יְאוֹרֵי דְמֵיהֶם,   וְדִמְעוֹת פְּנֵיהֶם,
לֹא תִשָּׁכַחְנָה לָנֶצַח.
כָּל חִיל וּגְנִיחָה,   וְנֶהִי צְרִיחָה,
מִשְּׁדוּדֵי לַהֲקוֹת הַכְּלָבִים,
זְכֹר וּסְפֹר,   בְּנֹאדְךָ צְרוֹר,
עַד עֵת נְקֹם עֶלְבּוֹן עֲלוּבִים.
בְּמַחֲנוֹת הַפְּרָאִים,   כְּאֵב וּנְגָעִים,
וּפַחֲדֵי נְפָשׁוֹת עֲגוּמוֹת,
חֲרָפוֹת וּצְחוֹק,   כְּלִימּוֹת וָרֹק,
פִּצְעֵי הַכָּאוֹת אֵימוֹת.

For the princes of Torah, the pillars of tradition,
for the young flowers of the priesthood,
for the diligent scholars, the men teachers and women,
and the precious children in school.

The trusting daughters, the elderly grandparents,
and their offspring,
and the infants whom they bore, everyone —
including the myriads beloved in life,
not parted by death.

Seek out their blood when You take the count
of all the scattered, rent leaves, of every life perished
in the days of destruction and calamity —
six thousand times a thousand.
An entire third to be destroyed,
by the Blitzkrieg's fury,
of the cherished vineyards You dearly loved.
O Avenger of blood!
The memory of their misery, please
do not erase from the book You have written.

Remember the moans and tumultuous screams,
when they were herded for slaughter —
May the rivers of their blood
and the tears on their faces:
not be forgotten forever.

Every tremble, every groan, every piercing cry
of those torn asunder by hoards of dogs,
remember and count them,
collect them into Your flask,
Till the time the degraded ones' shame is avenged.

In the barbarian's camps
were pain and sickness,
the anguish of mortified souls;
insults and mockery, shame and spit,
searing wounds from horrible blows.

וְרָעָבוֹן, צִמָּאוֹן,   שִׁגָּעוֹן, עִצָּבוֹן,
וְכִשָּׁלוֹן נֶחֱשָׁלִים בְּלִי כֹחַ,
וְכָל נְאָקוֹת חָלָל,   מִכָּל יָחִיד אֻמְלָל,
חֲלִילָה לְךָ מִלִּשְׁכֹּחַ.

וְתִימְרוֹת עָשָׁן,   וְקִיטוֹר מִכִּבְשָׁן,
תִּלֵּי תִלִּים עֲצָמוֹת וְגִידִים,
וְחַדְרֵי הָרַעַל,   קוֹל שְׁאָגוֹת מַקְהֵל
הַנֶּחֱנָקִים תּוֹךְ תָּאֵי הָאֵדִים.

וְסִרְחוֹן גּוּפוֹת,   וּגְוִיּוֹת סְגוּפוֹת,
גְּלַל דְּמֵן אַדְמַת נוֹאָצִים,
אֵיךְ הָפְכוּ טוֹרְפֵיהֶם,   לִבְרִיַּת חֶלְבֵּיהֶם,
וְעוֹר אִישׁ לְקִשּׁוּטֵי הַנָּשִׁים.

וּקְרִיצַת אֶצְבָּעוֹת,   שֶׁל רָאשֵׁי הַפְּרָעוֹת,
לִימִין שֶׁעֲבוּר פֶּרֶךְ,   צַלְמָוֶת לִשְׂמֹאל.
וְאֵיךְ יָרוּ יְרִיּוֹת   עַל חוֹפְרֵי הַבּוֹרוֹת,
בְּיִסּוּרֵי חִבּוּט קֶבֶר דַּרְדְּרוֹם שְׁאוֹל.

אֵיךְ עִנּוּ אֲחָיוֹתֵינוּ,   וְסֵרְסוּ בְנוֹתֵינוּ,
כּוֹסוֹת תַּרְעֵלָה מִיְּדֵי רוֹפְאִים אַכְזָרִים.
וּפְלִיטֵי הַשְּׂרִידִים   בִּמְחִלּוֹת וּסְתָרִים,
וְטָמְיוֹן יְלָדִים בְּבָתֵּי שֶׁמֶר כְּמָרִים.

שֶׂה תָמִים לָעוֹלָה,   דַּם בְּנֵי הַגּוֹלָה,
הוֹי אֲרִיאֵל מְנֻבֶּלֶת חֲסִידֶיךָ,
צֹאן קָדָשִׁים מִי יִמְנֶה,   אֲשֶׁר אָשָׁם לֹא תֶכְבֶּה,
בְּחוּנֶיךָ הָיוּ מְקֻדְּשֵׁי שְׁמֶךָ.

בְּקוֹל שְׁמַע יִשְׂרָאֵל,   מָסְרוּ נֶפֶשׁ לָאֵל,
שֶׁהוּא יְאַסְּפֵם, וְעַד יוֹם אַחֲרוֹן
הִצְדִּיקוּ דִּין,   וְאַף אֲנִי מַאֲמִין
עָנוּ, וְשָׁרוּ שִׁירַת בִּטָּחוֹן.

Hunger, thirst, frenzy, sorrow,
the faint stumbling without any strength;
every death-rattle of every forlorn one,
far be it from You to forget.

The pillars of smoke, the fumes from furnace,
Piles and piles of bones and sinews,
poison-filled halls,
the roaring sound of the multitude,
choking in gas chamber.

The stench of the bodies, the tortured corpses,
fertilizers for the soil of the blasphemers.
How the tormentors turned
their fat into soap,
and human skin into feminine adornments.

[Remember] the finger motions
of the savage officers.
To the right — slave labor!
To the left — the shadow of death.
[Remember] how the sharpshooters shot
at those digging [their own] graves,
lowering them to the depths in the agony of the grave.

And how they afflicted our sisters
and mutilated our daughters,
doses of poison from sadistic doctors,
And fugitive survivors
in burrows and bunkers,
and the disappearance of children
in houses of apostasy, in monasteries.

Unblemished sheep, completely consumed,
the blood of the Diaspora's children,
Woe! O Ariel, for the corpses of your devout ones.
Who could count the sacred flock,
whose flame will never be extinguished,
Your tested ones were Sanctifiers of Your name.

With the cry of 'Shema Yisrael,'
they gave up their lives for God,
so that He might gather them in.
And until the very last day,
they justified His judgment,
and called out, 'I believe...'
and sang a song of trust.

וּבְכֵן נִשְׁאַר עַם, כְּיָתוֹם נִדְהָם,
בְּלִי קְבָרִים לְהִשְׁתַּטֵּחַ.
וְלֹא מַצֵּבוֹת, אֵיפֹה לִבְכּוֹת.
יְבָבוֹת לְכָב רוֹתֵחַ.

רַק נִסְכֵּי הַדָּם, אַזְכָּרוֹתָם,
תּוֹסְסִים בְּלִי שׁוֹכֵחַ,
וְהֲרֵי אִפְרֵי עֲקֵדָתָם,
תְּרוּמוֹת דְּשְׁנֵי מִזְבֵּחַ.

מִי יְמַלֵּל   צַעַר יִשְׂרָאֵל,
אֲשֶׁר דַּעְתּוֹ מִכְּאֵב נִטְרֶפֶת,
וּשְׁאֵרִית הַפְּאֵר, כִּמְעַט מִזְעֵיר,
וְאֵיךְ קוֹמָתָהּ הַיּוֹם נִכְפֶּפֶת.

אֵל חַי מְרַחֵם, עֲדָתְךָ נַחֵם,
אֲשֶׁר לְךָ מְאֹד נִכְסֶפֶת,
אוֹר חָדָשׁ תָּזְרִיחַ, קַרְנֵי הוֹד תַּצְמִיחַ,
וְרוּחַ אֱלֹהִים מְרַחֶפֶת.

*And now, a people is left,
bewildered as an orphan —
without graves at which to pray,
without tombstones
where to weep
the laments of emotion-filled hearts.*

*Only blood libations
are their memorials
boiling, unforgettable —
and the mounds of ashes from their Akeidah,
are tributes from the Altar's ashes.*

*Who can express
Israel's torment,
whose mind is frenzied by misery?
The remnants of its splendor
is a fraction of a bit,
how its pride is humbled today!*

*O Living God! Merciful One!
Comfort Your congregation
that yearns for You so mightily,
Let new light shine,
let rays of glory grow,
And may God's spirit hover.*

APPENDIX 9
Additional photographs of monuments
that were not available
when text was completed.

Austiler. Mt. Moriah.

Baranow. New Montefiore.

Belchetow. Mt. Hebron.

Baranowich. Wellwood.

Bodker.

Bochinia.
Wishnitz
Brigel.

Britchan.

Bialobrzegi. Passaic Cemetery.

Brohilover. Mt. Moriah.

Chyrow. Wellwood.

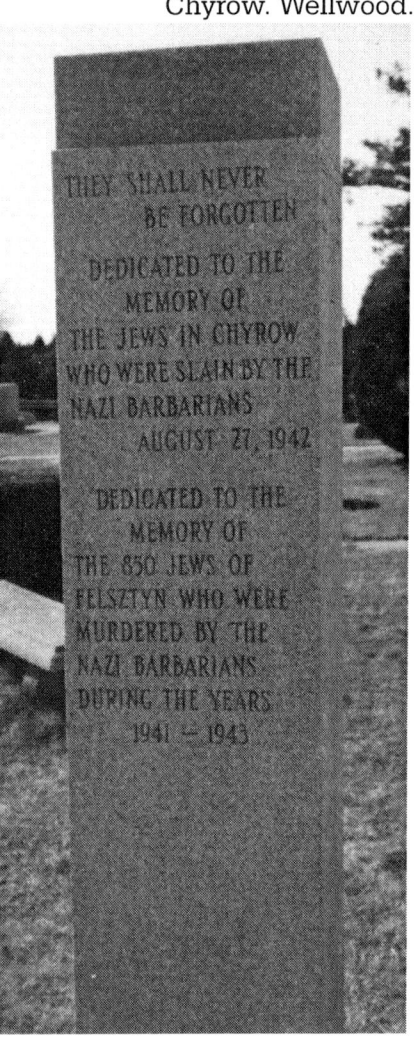

New Cracow. New Montefiore.

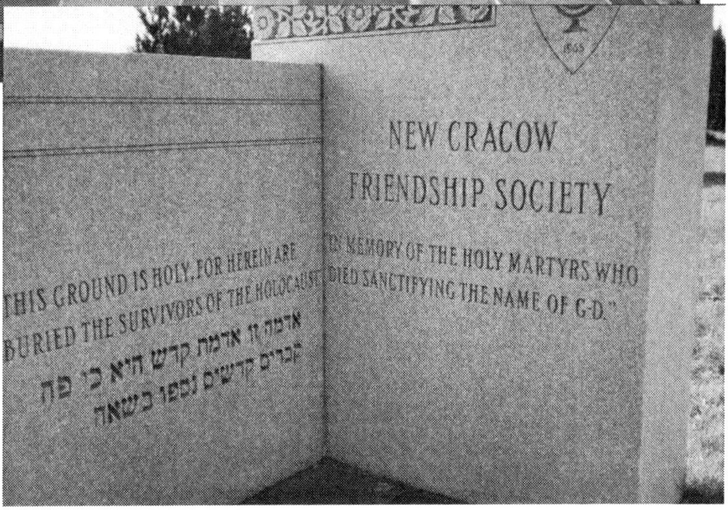

New Cracow. New Montefiore.

150

Dombier. New Montefiore.

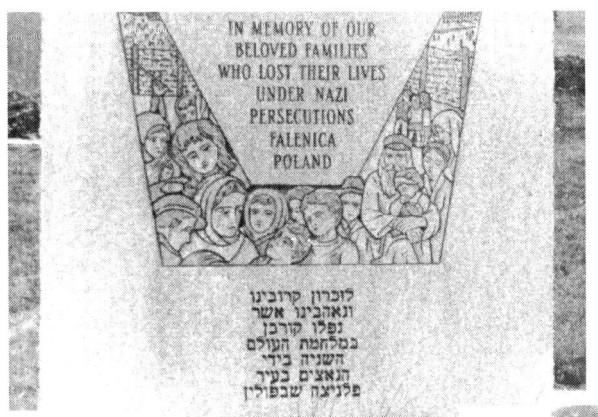

Falencia. Mt. Moriah.

Goniondz and Trestine. Beth El.

German Persecution Survivors.
Beth-El.

Jagielnicer. Mt. Hebron.

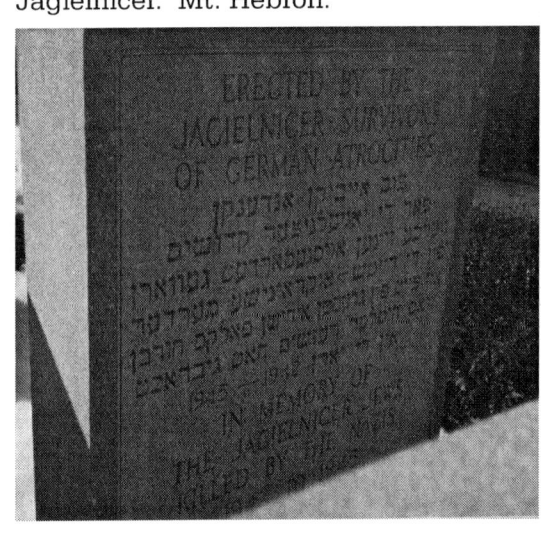

Grabower.
New Montefiore.

Kalushin. United Hebrew.

Krashnik.
New Montefiore.

Konstantin. New Montefiore.

Kuniver. New Montefiore.

Libovner Voliner. United Hebrew.

KORELITZER SOCIETY INC

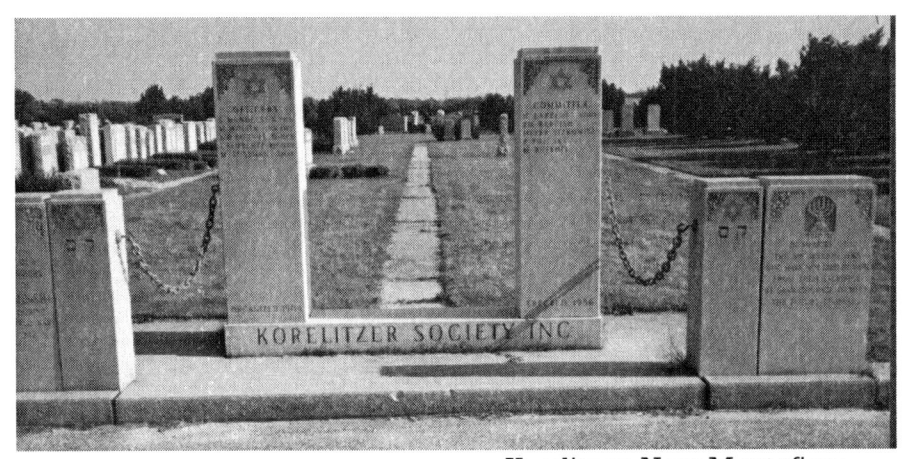

Korelitzer. New Montefiore.

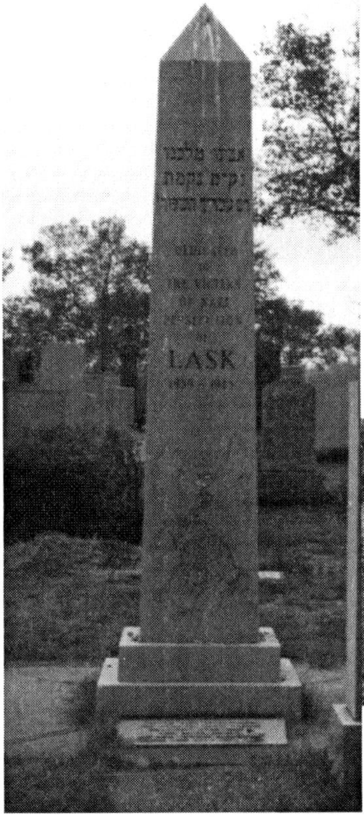
LASK

Lask. Beth David.

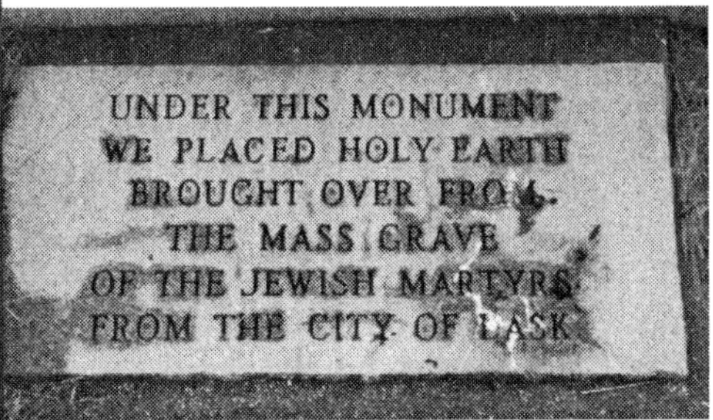
UNDER THIS MONUMENT
WE PLACED HOLY EARTH
BROUGHT OVER FROM
THE MASS GRAVE
OF THE JEWISH MARTYRS
FROM THE CITY OF LASK

Luber. New Montefiore.

Magiev. Beth Moses.

Moscisker. New Montefiore.

Lukower.

Grybower.

Tarnov.

Zamosc. Beth-El.

Apter (Opatow).

Jewish War Veterans.

Przemysl.

45 Kieltzer Children.

Kieltzer Children. Beth David.

Paviancer. Mt. Moriah.

Podhajce. Mt. Zion.

Plonsk. Beth David.

Miechover. New Montefiore.

Medgibosh. Beth David.

Ostrowcer. Beth David.

Skoler.

Lodzer.

Budzanower.

Radomer, New Montefiore.

Ducor. Cedar Park.

Husiatyner.

Pechowitz.

Radomer. New Montefiore.

Melnice. New Montefiore.

Ozorkower.
Passaic Juntion,
Passaic, NJ

Radomer. New Montefiore.

Radomer.

Skerniewice. Mt. Moriah.

Sokolover-Lejensker. Mt. Zion.

Sokolov Podlaski. New Montefiore.

Tchudnow. Beth David.

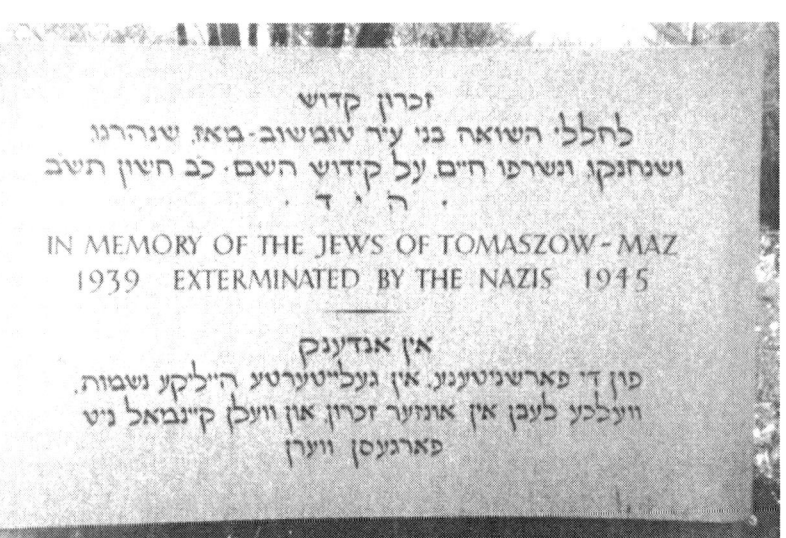

Tomaszow.
Beth-El.

Tyszowitzer.
United Hebrew.

Trzebinia.

Wladower. New Montefiore.

Yugoslav Jews.
Mt. Moriah.

B'nai Israel
Washington Heights.
Beth-El.

Zamosc.
Beth-El.

IN MEMORIAM

THIS MEMORIAL ERECTED IN MEMORY OF
TWELVE THOUSAND INNOCENT VICTIMS OF THE
CITY ZAMOSC POLAND WHO WERE BRUTALLY
BURNED GASSED AND SLAIN BY THE ABOMINABLE
NAZIS AND THEIR HELPERS IN THE YEARS OF
1939 ——— 1945
THEIR SACRED MEMORY WILL ALWAYS BE
ENSHRINED IN OUR HEARTS
WE WILL ALWAYS REMEMBER THEM
WE SHALL NEVER FORGET
WE SHALL NEVER FORGIVE
IN EVERLASTING MEMORY
WITH A DEEP SENSE OF PAINFUL FEELING, WE
SHALL NEVER FORGET FOR ONE MOMENT THE
EXTINGUISHED LIVES WHOSE NAMES WE DO NOT
KNOW AND THROUGH VARIOUS CIRCUMSTANCES
IT WAS NOT POSSIBLE TO MEMORIALIZE THEIR
NAMES ON THIS MONUMENT.
HONOR THEIR HOLY MEMORY

Krystynopoler.
Old Montefiore.

Shershow.
New Montefiore.

Rozdol. Mt. Hebron.

Eishishok.
United Hebrew.

Schachter Family. Beth David, Elmont, L.I.

SELECTED BIBLIOGRAPHY

ANTHOLOGY OF HOLOCAUST LITERATURE, Glatstein, Knox, Margoshes, Jewish Publication Society, 1973, pp. 329—331.
ANTIPOL YIZKOR BOOK, Ayalon, B.H. Tel Aviv, 1962.
BLACK BOOK OF POLISH JEWRY, Apenszlak, et al, American Federation for Polish Jews, N.Y., 1943.
HASHOAH U'SFEE-CHEHA, B'SFORIM HO-EEV-REE-IM, Piekarz, Mendel, Yad Vashem, Jerusalem, 1974.
HO-AYOROH B'LAHAVOS
  Sefer Zikoron L'keheelas Olkinik, Shlomo Farber, Tel Aviv, 1972
KEHILAS ROHATYN V'HA-SVEEVOH: IR B'CHAYEHO U-V'CHEELYONEHOH, Amiti, M. Tel Aviv, 1962, pp. 336-341.
KIDDUSH HASHEM, Weiss, Chana. Tel Aviv.
KOL D'MAY ACHIM:T'UDOS MAY-GHETO-OS, Tel Aviv, 1953.
LANZUT-CHAYEHO V'CHURBONOH SHEL K'HILAS Y'HUDIS, Weltzer-Kudish, Tel Aviv, 1963.
MATZEVAS ZIKORON LEE-K'DOSHAY K'HEELAS YAVOROV, Druch, S. NY, 1950.
MARTYRS AND FIGHTERS, Friedman-Praeger, NY, 1954, pp. 272-277.
NOTES FROM THE WARSAW GHETTO, Ringelbaum, Emanuel. McGraw-Hill, NY, 1958.
OHRIM V'EEMOHOS B'YISROEL, Vol. 2, Fishman, Rabbi YehudaLeib, Mosad Harav Kook, Jerusalem, 1958.
PINKAS BENDIN, Stein, A.M. Tel Aviv, 1958.
PINKAS HRUBIESHOW: Lee-m'los 20 Shonoh L'churban eer Moladetaynu, Kaplinsky, B. Tel Aviv, 1962.
PINKAS KOLBUSHOV, Biderman, New York, 1951
PINKAS LUDMIR-SEFER ZIKORON LEE-K'HEELAS LUDMIR, Tel Aviv, 1961.
PINKAS ZIKORON L'VOH-TAY ALMIN SHE-NE-HERSU V'CHOL'LU B'SHNOS HASHOAH, Prager, M. Tel Aviv, 1973.
PINKAS ZINKOV, Tel Aviv, 1955, (p. 4 speech at dedication), (p. 222 photo of monument).
RADOM, Stein, A.S. Tel Aviv, 1961, pp. LI, LII, LIII.
RADOMISHEL RABOSI V'HA-S'VEE-VOH, Harshoshanim et al, Tel Aviv,1970.
SEFER CRACOW: IR V'AYM B'YISROEL, Bauminger, Mosad Harav Kook, Jerusalem, 1959.
SEFER HAZIKORON L'ARTZOS HA-GOLAH-SIDRAS POlLEN, Jerusalem, 1952, pp. 603-650 Warsaw Ghetto.
SEFER HAZIKORON L'HEELAS SOSNOVITZ V'HA-S'VEE-VOH, Tel Aviv, 1963.
SEFER HAZIKORON LEE-K'HEELAS OSTROV-MEZUBAITSK, Gordon, A. Tel Aviv, 1953.
SEFER K'DOSHIM LEE-K'DOSHAY VISHNEWITZ SHE-NISFU B'SHO-AS HA-NATZIM, Rabin, C., Tel Aviv, 1971.

SEFER K'HEELAS Y'HUDAY DOMBROVA, Tel Aviv, 1950.
SEFER K'HEELAS ZLOTZOV, Krau, B., Tel Aviv, 1954.
SEFER KIELTZ, Tzitrin, P., Tel Aviv, 1957,
    (pp. 226-33 and pp. 235-252, Pogrom after War).
SEFER KOBRIN-M'GILAS CHAYIM V'CHURBON,
    Schwartz-Bilski, Tel Aviv, 1951.
SEFER KOSSOV, Kersei-Alitzki, Tel Aviv, 1957.
SEFER RYPIN, Kantz, S., Tel Aviv, 1957.
SEFER STASHUV V'HA-SVEE-VOH-PLANCH, Tel Aviv, 1962.
SEFER ZIKORON L'DROHOVITZ-BORYSLAV V'HA-SVEE-VOH,
    Gelber, N.M., Tel Aviv, 1958.
SEFER ZIKORON LIK'HEELOH DISNA,
    Bernstein-Zirlin, Tel Aviv, 1969.
SEFER ZIKORON L'KEHEELAS HORODOK
    Moshe Simon, Tel Aviv, 1963
SEFER WLADOMIRZ-GAL V'AYD L'ZAYCHER EE-RAY-NU,
    Marovitz, A., Tel Aviv, 1958.
STOLIN-SEFER ZIKORON L'KEHEELAS STOLIN V' HA-SVEE VOH,
    Avtichi-ben Zakai, Tel Aviv, 1953.
TIFEH VORTZLEN-FUN SASSOV BIZ YERUSHALAYIM,
    Zeigler, M., Tel Aviv, 1981, (pp. 424-7 photos of monument).
VENEZIA-OHRIM V'EE-MA-HOS B'YISRAEL,
    Maimon, Rabbi Y.L., Mosad Harav Kook, Jerusalem, 195 , pp. 55-88.
YAHADUS LITA, Hotzo-os am ha-Sefer, Tel Aviv, 1959.
ZDUNSKA-WOLA,Ehrlich, A., Tel Aviv, 1968, (p. 27, photo of monument).

ABOUT THE AUTHOR

Rabbi Alvin M. Poplack was ordained at the Rabbinical Academy of Mesivta Chaim Berlin in 1944, and has held pulpits in Medford, Massachusetts and Lebanon, Pennsylvania. He was the spiritual leader of the Bellerose Jewish Center in Floral Park, New York from 1956 to 1986, when he retired as Rabbi Emeritus. During his tenure, he served the greater Jewish community in many ways: as President of the Long Island Commission of Rabbis, as Chairman of the Queens Council for Soviet Jewry and as Secretary of the New York Board of Rabbis, among other positions of leadership.

Rabbi Poplack holds a B.A. from Lebanon Valley College, a Master's in Religious Education from Yeshiva University and a Doctorate in Jewish Literature from the Jewish Teachers Seminary/Touro College in New York.

Upon retiring from his pulpit, Rabbi Poplack was appointed Chaplain of the International Synagogue at JFK Airport in New York, where he served for fifteen years. He retired in 2001 as the senior chaplain of the airport's chaplain corps, as well as a senior chaplain of the Port Authority Police, with the rank of Inspector.

Rabbi Poplack is married to the former Rosalind Schacter. They are the parents of three children and grandparents of four. They recently moved to Florida, where they reside in Pembroke Pines.